Interactive
Whiteboards

30 Activities to Engage All Learners

Made Easy

Getting Started

Comprehension

Aa Bb Vocabulary Development

Activating Prior Knowledge

Graphic Organizers

Author

Mark Murphy

SHELL EDUCATION

Publishing Credits

Dona Herweck Rice, *Editor-in-Chief*; Lee Aucoin, *Creative Director*; Don Tran, *Print Production Manager*; Timothy J. Bradley, *Illustration Manager*; Sara Johnson, *Senior Editor*; Hillary Wolfe, *Editor*; James Anderson, *Associate Editor*; Robin Erickson, *Cover Designer/Interior Layout Designer*; Stephanie Reid, *Cover Photographer*; Corinne Burton, M.A. Ed., *Publisher*

Shell Education

5301 Oceanus Drive
Huntington Beach, CA 92649-1030
http://www.shelleducation.com
ISBN 978-1-4258-0682-8
©2011 Shell Educational Publishing, Inc.

Table of Contents

Research and Introduction

Teachers and Students in the 21st Century

If you are a teacher right now, chances are that you remember having basal readers in elementary school, then, in middle and high school, lugging around English, mathematics, science, and history textbooks. Today's students might characterize the way you learned as "so last century"—and they would be right. Today's students are living and learning in the 21st century, and the way things used to be done is "history."

Gone are the days when students were individual, passive learners of facts and formulas. The students of today are collaborative, active learners who need to know where and how to get information from more than just memorizing and storing details from a single source, such as a textbook (Magaña and Frenkel 2009).

The teacher's role has transformed as well. Rather than being *disseminators*, modern teachers need to be *facilitators*. Students today are using the latest technology outside of school to entertain themselves, connect with friends, and instantly find information about anything that interests them. It only makes sense to use these tools in their classrooms, as well—under the guidance of a skilled teacher. In reality, few teachers have implemented the use of Web 2.0 applications, tools, podcasts, blogs, or wikis in their classrooms—perhaps because learning and using these technological tools seems daunting to those teachers who have not used these materials themselves. Yet educators who intend to continue teaching in

the 21st century must begin to take steps toward technological literacy. One step that is effective and not too far beyond even a reluctant teacher's comfort zone is the use of interactive whiteboards as a teaching and learning tool.

Why Use Interactive Whiteboards?

In an article published in the November 2009 issue of *Educational Leadership*, Robert Marzano offers this conclusion based on research (Becker and Lee) regarding the use of interactive whiteboards in the classroom:

> "The study results indicated that, in general, using interactive whiteboards was associated with a 16 percentile point gain in student achievement. This means that we can expect a student at the 50th percentile in a classroom without the technology to increase to the 66th percentile in a classroom using whiteboards."

Marzano also predicts that the use of interactive whiteboards will "grow exponentially" and that "books like The Interactive Whiteboard Revolution (Becker and Lee 2009) attest to the depth and breadth of change this tool can promote in classroom practice."

How Are Interactive Whiteboards Different from Regular Whiteboards?

In the last 20 years, chalkboards were replaced with whiteboards. The only difference was material; the method of delivery was the same. The teacher wrote on the board any information that was used in the lesson, and then it was erased. In this century, interactive whiteboards are replacing traditional whiteboards, and the difference is radical in both material and delivery. An interactive whiteboard is a large display that is connected to a computer. The computer's screen is projected onto the display board where information is not only seen by the whole group, but can also be manipulated in real time. Lessons can include elements that could have never been shown on a traditional chalkboard or whiteboard, and anything displayed, changed, or written on an interactive whiteboard can be saved.

How Interactive Whiteboards Benefit Students

The 21st century classroom does have something in common with the classrooms of the past—that is, a diversity of students. In any given class, there may be high-achieving, average, low-performing, and struggling students. There may be students with low motivation to learn or high motivation to learn. There may be students whose first language is something other than English and students with special needs. Within these various groups will be students who have different learning modalities—visual, auditory, and tactile. Using interactive whiteboards can benefit all of these students (Beeland Jr. 2002; Torff and Tirotta 2010).

Interactive whiteboards...

- improve student participation
- increase motivation and engagement
- allow all students access to material and the ability to interact with it
- appeal to students at all levels of achievement
- help students focus and attend to lessons
- encourage student input and increase involvement
- provide opportunities for visual, auditory, and tactile experiences
- promote collaborative learning
- enhance exposure to various models of information and a variety of media
- give immediate feedback
- foster a sense of community in the classroom
- extend students' ability to access people and information outside the classroom
- afford the ability to save, print, and share lessons and notes

Teaching with Interactive Whiteboards— When More Is Less

Teaching and learning in recent years has been defined by standards, accountability, testing, and "leaving no child behind." The 21st century brings with it new challenges for teachers. Perhaps in the recent explosion of technology, you may feel as if it is you that is being left behind. First, if you are not a "techie," do not be discouraged. You can bring technology into your classroom one step at a time. Fortunately, using interactive whiteboards is a great way to do this. Do not fall into the trap of thinking that this is something more to add on top of your already-full workload. An interactive whiteboard is a tool that, in fact, does add more to your classroom by opening up a whole world of information, and can also mean less work for you. How? Consider these "more is less" time-saving features of using interactive whiteboards:

- If you are like most teachers, you have wasted time looking for lesson plans or notes you made for a previous lesson but finally ended up just redoing it. You probably have also wished that you had saved a lesson plan that worked particularly well, but it was lost once the lesson was over. Anything you do on an interactive whiteboard—from a prepared lesson and notes made right on the screen, to student-added input—can be saved, printed, and shared. A lesson on nouns that includes animated video and sound will be there next year when you want to teach the lesson again. Even if you are adept at saving your lesson plans and notes for future reference, interactive whiteboard lessons can capture the whole lesson, including

any multimedia components such as pictures, sound, and animation and are all ready to use again whenever you want.

- How much time do you think you have spent writing out notes on the board or charts, making student worksheets, study sheets, or handouts, or preparing homework assignments and providing makeup work for students who have missed class? Interactive whiteboards save what you have prepared and can provide the exact lesson to any student who missed class or just needs a review. You can print out any or all parts of a lesson (without taking the time and resources to make photocopies), or they can be shared electronically.

- Perhaps the greatest time-saver created by interactive whiteboard lessons is in removing the constraints of independent lesson preparation. You can share interactive whiteboard lessons with colleagues—not just with teachers in your school, but around the country or even the world. Why reinvent the wheel when you can connect with other teachers who have been there, done that?

If interactive whiteboards are new to you, this book is a great place to start. You will find ready-made, easy-to-implement lessons across the curriculum. There are six sections with five activities per section, one in each of these five content areas: mathematics, science, social studies, reading, and writing. Once you have tried these lessons and seen for yourself how engaged and responsive your students can be, you will be "sold" on using this technology in the classroom.

Getting the Most from Interactive Whiteboards

Think of the interactive whiteboard as a tool with many versatile functions. At its most basic level, it can function as an electronic projector. However, limiting its use to this function would be like hiring a symphony and then asking only one musician to play! To get the most out of this technology and its multiple capabilities, you may want to explore Web-based resources. Although interactive whiteboards are relatively new, there are already many sites that have been created for teachers who want to use this technology in their classrooms. These sites range from sponsored sites to teacher networks. There is a large amount of supportive material—much of it free—including quite a bit of software. It is easy to find almost anything you might want to use in your classroom. Although much of the resource materials are classroom-quality, you will, of course, want to scrutinize each source before using any with students. There are even sites to help you weed through the vast resources available online. A good place to find guidance is your state's education website, which may direct you to any number of pre-screened and recommended resources. You can also join a teacher network where you can share information, reviews, and lessons with other teachers. Of course, many Shell Education products include interactive whiteboard compatible materials, as well!

These activities are helpful as you build your confidence and skill using the interactive whiteboard over time, but what if you just need something on the fly—maybe before or even during a lesson? How do you find something

appropriate without wading through dozens of Web entries? The key is to enter specific search words in your preferred search engine and then scan the promising entries that appear and evaluate the sources. This can be done quickly, as seen in the following example:

> During Mr. Haas' science lesson about the human body, a student asks how the heart pumps blood. In a matter of seconds, Mr. Haas can find several resources online that illustrate this, choose an appropriate one, download it, and display it. First, Mr. Haas types the key words *heart pumping* into the search bar engine of his Web browser. Several links are listed. He skims through them. Of the first five links, he sees two that may be appropriate for his demonstration. The other links have to do with transplants and heart pumps. Of the two links that claim to be animated videos of a pumping heart, Mr. Haas glances at the sources. One is **http://yourdoctor.com** and the other is **http://health.nih.gov/** and, although either link may be appropriate, Mr. Haas chooses the National Institutes of Health site to be certain. When he opens the site, he is pleased to see exactly what he needs. He can then project the video on the interactive whiteboard for all students to watch.

Getting the Most from
Interactive Whiteboards *(cont.)*

If you have ever done a search on your Web browser, you know that finding what you want is not always that easy. Keep in mind that you greatly improve your chances of quickly locating quality resources by entering specific, narrow search terms and then examining the sources of the results. Many sources are easily questionable—they may or may not be accurate or appropriate. Others, such as government agencies, libraries, universities, museums, and reputable organizations or foundations, are better bets. Although, if you cannot identify a source from its abbreviation in a listing, look for the suffixes *.gov* (government) or *.edu* (education) in Web addresses. If the topic appears to be what you need, but you are unsure of its origin, you can always open it to check the content and the source. ***Note:*** As a teacher, always be concerned about the quality and the appropriateness of any content students might see or access over the Internet. Teaching students how to screen searches is a very valuable and necessary part of using computers in the classroom. In the example of Mr. Haas, he could have used his search as a model and walked the students through his screening process.

Here are more tips about Internet resources:

- If you are looking for a fun activity, add the words *game*, *fun*, or *puzzle* to the search term, such as "multiplication fact *fun*" or "state capital *puzzle*."
- If you are looking for an illustration, specify *photo*, *drawing*, *graph*, or *painting* in your search options.

Finally, keep in mind that, while you can easily download images, sounds, video, articles, and a host of other things, you and your students are required to abide by copyright and fair use laws and restrictions. Again, teachers can model this by demonstrating where and how to find copyright information on websites and postings. Impress upon students that they must be responsible, good-members-in-standing of the digital community.

Organization and Management

Adapting to Interactive Whiteboards

As a teacher, you are already skilled in organization and management. Adapting to using online resources and interactive whiteboards should be just a matter of shifting from the "paper" world to the "digital" world. In many ways, organization of digital files is easier (and certainly more compact) than handling physical stacks of books, lessons, resources, and records. Generally, you will want to save files and organize them in folders in much the same way you do on your home computer. However, there are a few tips to follow and pitfalls to avoid.

- **Do not put any personal information or files on the computer you use at school.** If possible, make this a dedicated computer on which only school lessons and other non-sensitive files are kept. Even if you do not share your school computer or intend to share files with colleagues, treat the computer as if anything on it could be seen by anyone without any cause for concern. This includes any identifying information about yourself or your students, such as last names or email addresses.

- **Be meticulous about naming your files.** Although you may have files on your personal computer labeled "Joe's Vacation Pictures," you will want to be very precise and specific when naming your files for school use. If possible, include tags that could be picked up as keywords in a search. For example, a file named "LStundras" may have seemed perfectly clear when you taught tundras in Life Science, but even if you do remember the name, it is not very "searchable." A better choice would be "Life Science Gr. 7 tundra IWB lesson with photos." Then, if you or another teacher with whom you are collaborating look for any of these key words (e.g., *tundra, life science, IWB lesson, Gr. 7, photos of tundra, science Gr. 7, Gr. 7 tundra,* and so on) your lesson will be the immediate result of that search.

- **Avoid saving too many files.** A common pitfall when working with files is to save several versions of the same file. You may want to do this while you are working on a project, but once it is done, delete the older versions. If you do want to save different versions of a lesson, for example, the same lesson differentiated for an advanced group and an ELL class, be sure to label each one clearly.

Teacher Versus Machine— How to Win

Teachers are responsible for managing all operations. Using the interactive whiteboard is clearly more complex than using a piece of chalk or a dry-erase marker. First, you will notice that instead of having to have your back to the class as you write on the board or chart, you can now face the group (and monitor their behavior, attentiveness, reactions, and responses). You will still need to manage the equipment, but you will no longer need to have "eyes in the back of your head." If you fear that technology may defeat you by not doing what you want or expect, take heart. In the struggle of teacher versus machine, you can take steps to ensure that you win.

1. Leave lots of space around the whiteboard—in front and to the sides—to allow access without blocking the beam.

2. Make sure that the whiteboard is mounted high enough for everyone to see but low enough for students to touch. (For young students, provide a stool or a long-handled pointer. Some students benefit by using a tennis ball instead of their fingers.)

3. Place the computer or keyboard near the whiteboard so that text can be added without constantly having to move across the classroom to access input.

4. Check the sound level and quality of the speaker. If it is insufficient for your needs, add external speakers.

5. Use electrical tape to secure the cord to avoid tripping.

6. If the equipment is on a cart, place it in an area where it is not likely to get bumped or jarred.

7. Set the screen resolution to 1024 x 768, and choose fonts and sizes that can easily be seen from the farthest point in the room. Avoid white or pale colors. To reduce glare from windows, improve the contrast of the material on the screen by using dark backgrounds with white or light-colored text and graphics.

8. Whenever possible, create documents that fit "as is" on the screen. In other words, add page breaks to avoid having to scroll up and down. Include an end-of-page marker, and keep tools at the top of the page. Use full-screen or presentation mode to show the entire page.

9. In any application, make use of the "floating" tools provided, such as highlighters and colored pens.

10. When projecting a website, use the full-screen function.
    Tip: In Internet Explorer, press F11 to remove all toolbars from view. In *Safari*, click **Command**+**Shift**+\. Doing this will eliminate unnecessary distractions and allow the page to display larger.

What Can You Do With an Interactive Whiteboard?

The lessons and activities in this book are good starting points for implementing the use of interactive whiteboards in the classroom. As you become more comfortable using this technology, you may want to save a duplicate copy and adapt the activities to place your own content and ideas into them. In addition to these activities, there are other things that you can do with interactive whiteboards. With an interactive whiteboard, anything you can create or view on a computer can be displayed, manipulated, saved, shared, or printed. The possibilities are endless. Here are just a few ideas for using interactive whiteboards with large or small groups:

• ***PowerPoint*® presentations** These can be teacher-made or student-created projects.	• **Group analysis and critical thinking** Project a piece of literature to discuss, student-written stories to read and share, or a reader's theater script to perform.
• **Interactive worksheets** Use these for guided practice, demonstration, or review.	• **Primary sources** Share original documents, music, art, and so on. (Check copyrights for intended use beyond viewing.) Play videos of interviews, news clips, documentaries, and so on.
• **Graphic organizers** In addition to the ones provided in this book, you can tap into dozens more that are topic specific or open-ended. You can also create and save your own.	• **Interactive multimedia** Make any presentation interactive and multimedia by adding pictures, sounds, commentaries, highlighting, captions, and notes.
• **Previewing and practice** Preview a lesson by displaying a picture or excerpt and hear students' responses to determine prior knowledge. Display practice tests to work on together or demonstrate how to complete test items or directions.	• **Publish and share student work** Encourage students to share the products of their efforts: stories and other written pieces, projects, research results, original artwork, and so on.
• **Prewriting activities** Project brainstorming sessions, note-taking ideas, sentence starters, grammar rules, pictures to stimulate discussions or to prompt writing, and so on.	• **Post class information** Display notices, calendars, schedules, homework assignments, and more.

How to Use This Book

The *Interactive Whiteboards Made Easy* series was created to provide teachers with model activities for integrating interactive whiteboard technology into their instruction. The activities are meant to show how easily interactive whiteboards can be used across the content areas of mathematics, science, social studies, reading, and writing to enhance instruction and complement lessons that are already in place within the core curriculum. The information on pages 12–15 outlines the major components and purposes for each activity.

Activity Plan

The standard provided here includes the content-area objective of the activity.

The tab describes the activity section: Getting Started Activities, Vocabulary Development Activities, Activating Prior Knowledge Activities, Graphic Organizer Activities, Comprehension Activities, and Review Activities.

The file name, title, and page number of the student activity sheet, as well as any additional materials necessary to complete the activity are listed here.

The interactive whiteboard skills used in the activity are outlined here. Review those skills using the How-to Guide found on pages 119–124.

Within the procedure section, the interactive whiteboard skills are boldfaced to call attention to when they are used.

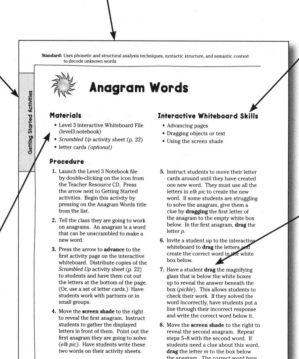

Standard: Uses phonetic and structural analysis techniques, syntactic structure, and semantic context to decode unknown words

Getting Started Activities

Anagram Words

Materials
- Level 3 Interactive Whiteboard File (level3.notebook)
- *Scrambled Up* activity sheet (p. 22)
- letter cards *(optional)*

Interactive Whiteboard Skills
- Advancing pages
- Dragging objects or text
- Using the screen shade

Procedure
1. Launch the Level 3 Notebook file by double-clicking on the icon from the Teacher Resource CD. Press the arrow next to Getting Started activities. Begin this activity by pressing on the Anagram Words title from the list.
2. Tell the class they are going to work on anagrams. An anagram is a word that can be unscrambled to make a new word.
3. Press the arrow to **advance** to the first activity page on the interactive whiteboard. Distribute copies of the *Scrambled Up* activity sheet (p. 22) to students and have them cut out the letters at the bottom of the page. (Or, use a set of letter cards.) Have students work with partners or in small groups.
4. Move the **screen shade** to the right to reveal the first anagram. Instruct students to gather the displayed letters in front of them. Point out the first anagram they are going to solve (*elk pic*). Have students write these two words on their activity sheets.
5. Instruct students to move their letter cards around until they have created one new word. They must use all the letters in *elk pic* to create the new word. If some students are struggling to solve the anagram, give them a clue by **dragging** the first letter of the anagram to the empty white box below. In the first anagram, **drag** the letter *p*.
6. Invite a student up to the interactive whiteboard to **drag** the letters and create the correct word in the white box below.
7. Have a student **drag** the magnifying glass that is below the white boxes up to reveal the answer beneath the box (*pickle*). This allows students to check their work. If they solved the word incorrectly, have students put a line through their incorrect response and write the correct word below it.
8. Move the **screen shade** to the right to reveal the second anagram. Repeat steps 5–8 with the second word. If students need a clue about this word, **drag** the letter *m* to the box below the anagram. The correct word here is *mustard*.

20 #50682—*Interactive Whiteboards Made Easy: Level 3* © Shell Education

Activity Plan *(cont.)*

The icon represents the section in which this activity belongs. It corresponds to the information found on the tab on the edge of the page.

Additional lesson ideas are included that link the activity to content-area instruction.

A sample of the interactive whiteboard files for each activity are shown here to help teachers visualize how to complete the activity before practicing with the actual file.

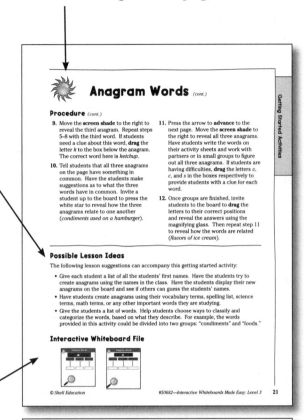

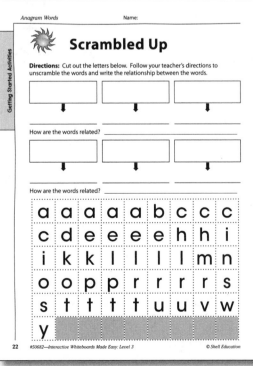

The student activity sheet mirrors the interactive whiteboard page, allowing all students to participate in the activity, even if they are not at the actual board. The activity sheet can also be used for formative assessment.

Teacher Resource CD

The Teacher Resource CD provided with this book contains electronic copies of all of the student reproducible activity sheets. It also contains the interactive whiteboard files that are used with each activity. In addition, teacher-planning resources are included. (See p. 128 for detailed information on the CD.)

Here are some general system requirements: For Mac®, Power PC® G3 500 MHz or faster processor, or Intel® 1.33 GHz or faster processor, 128 MB of RAM. For PC, Windows® Intel® Pentium® II 450 GHz or faster processor, 128 MB of RAM.

Integrating This Resource into Your Curriculum

When planning instruction using this resource, it is important to look ahead at your instructional time line and daily lesson plans to see where the activities provided in *Interactive Whiteboards Made Easy* can best be integrated. The Content-Area Matrix (p. 118) and the Standards Correlation (pp. 16–17) are two resources that can help you choose which activities will best fit your planned curriculum. Preview the activities to find one that correlates with the objective listed in your time line. The *Instructional Time Line* template (p. 15) is provided to help integrate this resource into long-range planning.

Implementing the Activities

After integrating this resource into your instructional time line, use the steps below to help you implement the activities.

1. Familiarize yourself with the written activity. Use the thumbnail image of the interactive whiteboard pages to visualize how the steps may take place while conducting the activity.

2. Review the Interactive Whiteboard Skills section of the lesson. Make sure you are comfortable with all of the skills necessary to conduct the lesson. If review is needed, look at the How-to Guide (pp. 119–124) sections that correspond with those required skills.

3. Open the interactive whiteboard file that accompanies the activity. Practice the activity to make sure you are comfortable with the necessary interactive whiteboard skills and how to use the pages to enhance your instruction.

4. If desired, invite a colleague to watch you practice delivering instruction of some or all of the activity. The technology becomes easier to use the more often you practice!

Instructional Time Line

Directions: In the first column, record the date of the lesson. In the second column, record the standards and/or objectives to be taught with that lesson. In the third column, write a brief description of the lesson to be taught. In the fourth and fifth columns, write the *Interactive Whiteboards Made Easy* activities and page numbers to be used to support the lesson. In the sixth column, include any adaptations or notes regarding the activities and/or lessons.

Instructional Time Line					
Date	Standard/ Objective	Lesson Description	Interactive Whiteboards Made Easy Activity	Pages	Adaptations or Notes

Standards Correlation

Shell Education is committed to producing educational materials that are research and standards based. In this effort, we have correlated all of our products to the academic standards of all 50 states, the District of Columbia, and the Department of Defense Dependent Schools.

How to Find Standards Correlations

To print a customized correlation report of this product for your state, visit our website at **http://www.shelleducation. com** and follow the on-screen directions. If you require assistance in printing correlation reports, please contact Customer Service at 1-877-777-3450.

Purpose and Intent of Standards

The No Child Left Behind legislation mandates that all states adopt academic standards that identify the skills students will learn in kindergarten through grade twelve. While many states had already adopted academic standards prior to NCLB, the legislation set requirements to ensure the standards were detailed and comprehensive.

Standards are designed to focus instruction and guide adoption of curricula. Standards are statements that describe the criteria necessary for students to meet specific academic goals. They define the knowledge, skills, and content students should acquire at each level. Standards are also used to develop standardized tests to evaluate students' academic progress.

Teachers are required to demonstrate how their lessons meet state standards. State standards are used in development of all of our products, so educators can be assured they meet the academic requirements of each state.

McREL Compendium

We use the Mid-continent Research for Education and Learning (McREL) Compendium to create standards correlations. Each year, McREL analyzes state standards and revises the compendium. By following this procedure, McREL is able to produce a general compilation of national standards. Each lesson in this product is based on one or more McREL standards. The chart on the following page lists each standard taught in this product and the page numbers for the corresponding lessons.

TESOL Standards

The lessons in this book promote English language development for English language learners. The standards listed on page 18 support the language objectives presented throughout the lessons.

Lesson Title	Content Area	Standard
Anagram Words (pp. 20–22)	Reading	Uses phonetic and structural analysis techniques, syntactic structure, and semantic context to decode unknown words
Analogies (pp. 23–25)	Science	Knows that living organisms have distinct structures and body systems that serve specific functions in growth, survival, and reproduction
Calendar (pp. 26–28)	Writing	Writes in order to communicate ideas and inform

Lesson Title	Content Area	Standard
Daily Geography (pp. (29–31)	Social Studies	Understands the characteristics and uses of maps, globes, and other geographic tools and technologies
Daily Mathematics (pp. 32–34)	Mathematics	Understands and applies basic and advanced properties of the concepts of numbers
Alike and Different (pp. 35–37)	Reading	Uses the various parts of a book (e.g., index, table of contents, glossary, appendix, preface) to locate information
Concept of Definition Map (pp. 38–40)	Social Studies	Understands how stories, legends, songs, ballads, games, and tall tales describe the environment, lifestyles, beliefs, and struggles of people in various regions
Example/Nonexample (pp. 41–43)	Science	Knows matter has three forms: solid, liquid, and gas
Total Physical Response (pp. 44–46)	Mathematics	Understands and applies basic and advanced properties of the concepts of geometry
Word Tiles (pp. 47–49)	Writing	Uses prefixes in written compositions
Analyze the Picture (pp. 50–52)	Social Studies	Understands changes in activities in the local community since its founding
Anticipation Guide (pp. 53–55)	Reading	Previews text
Historical Document (pp. 56–58)	Mathematics	Reads and interprets simple bar graphs
List, Group, Label (pp. 59–61)	Science	Understands atmospheric processes and the water cycle
Picture Predictions (pp. 62–64)	Writing	Uses adjectives in written compositions
Venn Diagram (pp. 65–67)	Writing	Uses prewriting strategies to plan written work
Flow Chart (pp. 68–70)	Reading	Understands structural patterns or organization in informational texts (e.g., chronological, logical, or sequential order)
KWL Chart (pp. 71–73)	Science	Knows the sun provides the light and heat necessary to maintain the temperature of Earth
T-Chart (pp. 74–76)	Mathematics	Understands the basic meaning of place value
Web Map (pp. 77–79)	Social Studies	Knows the characteristics of a variety of regions
Cause and Effect (pp. 80–82)	Social Studies	Understands how communities in North America varied long ago
Classify and Categorize (pp. 83–85)	Mathematics	Knows basic geometric language for describing and naming shapes
Main Idea and Details (pp. 86–88)	Science	Understands the composition and structure of the universe and Earth's place in it
Sequencing (pp. 89–91)	Reading	Understands the structural patterns and organization in informational texts
Summarizing (pp. 92–94)	Writing	Writes in response to literature
Content Links (pp. 95–97)	Science	Knows that plants and animals progress through the cycles of birth, growth and development, reproduction, and death
Game Board (pp. 98–100)	Writing	Uses grammatical and mechanical conventions in written compositions
Guess It! (pp. 101–103)	Social Studies	Knows the location of places, geographic features, and patterns in the environment
Question It! (pp. 104–106)	Mathematics	Uses basic and advanced procedures while performing the processes of computation
Draw and Guess (pp. 107–109)	Reading	Understands parts of speech

Tesol Standards

Lesson	Content Area	Standard
All lessons	All content areas	To use English to communicate in social settings: Students will use English to participate in social interactions
All lessons	All content areas	To use English to communicate in social settings: Students will interact in, through, and with spoken and written English for personal expression and enjoyment
All lessons	All content areas	To use English to communicate in social settings: Students will use learning strategies to extend their communicative competence
All lessons	All content areas	To use English to achieve academically in all content areas: Students will use English to interact in the classroom
All lessons	All content areas	To use English to achieve academically in all content areas: Students will use English to obtain, process, construct, and provide subject matter information in spoken and written form
All lessons	All content areas	To use English to achieve academically in all content areas: Students will use appropriate learning strategies to construct and apply academic knowledge
All lessons	All content areas	To use English in socially and culturally appropriate ways: Students will use the appropriate language variety, register, and genre according to audience, purpose, and setting
All lessons	All content areas	To use English in socially and culturally appropriate ways: Students will use nonverbal communication appropriate to audience, purpose, and setting
All lessons	All content areas	To use English in socially and culturally appropriate ways: Students will use appropriate learning strategies to extend their sociolinguistic and sociocultural competence

Notes

Anagram Words

Getting Started Activities

Materials

- Level 3 Interactive Whiteboard File (level3.notebook)
- *Scrambled Up* activity sheet (p. 22)
- letter cards *(optional)*

Procedure

1. Launch the Level 3 Notebook file by double-clicking on the icon from the Teacher Resource CD. Press the arrow next to Getting Started activities. Begin this activity by pressing on the Anagram Words title from the list.

2. Tell the class they are going to work on anagrams. An anagram is a word that can be unscrambled to make a new word.

3. Press the arrow to **advance** to the first activity page on the interactive whiteboard. Distribute copies of the *Scrambled Up* activity sheet (p. 22) to students and have them cut out the letters at the bottom of the page. (Or, use a set of letter cards.) Have students work with partners or in small groups.

4. Move the **screen shade** to the right to reveal the first anagram. Instruct students to gather the displayed letters in front of them. Point out the first anagram they are going to solve (*elk pic*). Have students write these two words on their activity sheets.

Interactive Whiteboard Skills

- Advancing pages
- Dragging objects or text
- Using the screen shade

5. Instruct students to move their letter cards around until they have created one new word. They must use all the letters in *elk pic* to create the new word. If some students are struggling to solve the anagram, give them a clue by **dragging** the first letter of the anagram to the empty white box below. In the first anagram, **drag** the letter *p*.

6. Invite a student up to the interactive whiteboard to **drag** the letters and create the correct word in the white box below.

7. Have a student **drag** the magnifying glass that is below the white boxes up to reveal the answer beneath the box (*pickle*). This allows students to check their work. If they solved the word incorrectly, have students put a line through their incorrect response and write the correct word below it.

8. Move the **screen shade** to the right to reveal the second anagram. Repeat steps 5–8 with the second word. If students need a clue about this word, **drag** the letter *m* to the box below the anagram. The correct word here is *mustard*.

Anagram Words *(cont.)*

Procedure *(cont.)*

9. Move the **screen shade** to the right to reveal the third anagram. Repeat steps 5–8 with the third word. If students need a clue about this word, **drag** the letter *k* to the box below the anagram. The correct word here is *ketchup*.

10. Tell students that all three anagrams on the page have something in common. Have the students make suggestions as to what the three words have in common. Invite a student up to the board to press the white star to reveal how the three anagrams relate to one another (*condiments used on a hamburger*).

11. Press the arrow to **advance** to the next page. Move the **screen shade** to the right to reveal all three anagrams. Have students write the words on their activity sheets and work with partners or in small groups to figure out all three anagrams. If students are having difficulties, **drag** the letters *v*, *c*, and *s* in the boxes respectively to provide students with a clue for each word.

12. Once groups are finished, invite students to the board to **drag** the letters to their correct positions and reveal the answers using the magnifying glass. Then repeat step 11 to reveal how the words are related (*flavors of ice cream*).

Possible Lesson Ideas

The following lesson suggestions can accompany this getting started activity:

- Give each student a list of all the students' first names. Have the students try to create anagrams using the names in the class. Have the students display their new anagrams on the board and see if others can guess the students' names.

- Have students create anagrams using their vocabulary terms, spelling list, science terms, math terms, or any other important words they are studying.

- Give the students a list of words. Help students choose ways to classify and categorize the words, based on what they describe. For example, the words provided in this activity could be divided into two groups: "condiments" and "foods."

Interactive Whiteboard File

Name:

Scrambled Up

Directions: Cut out the letters below. Follow your teacher's directions to unscramble the words and write the relationship between the words.

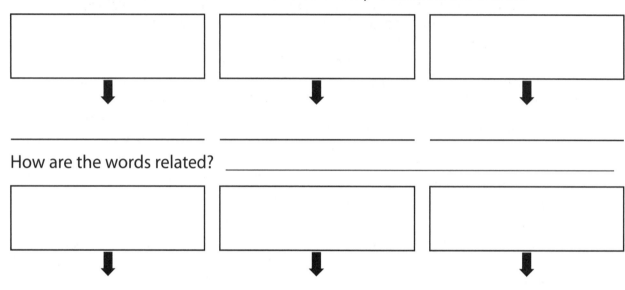

How are the words related? _____

How are the words related? _____

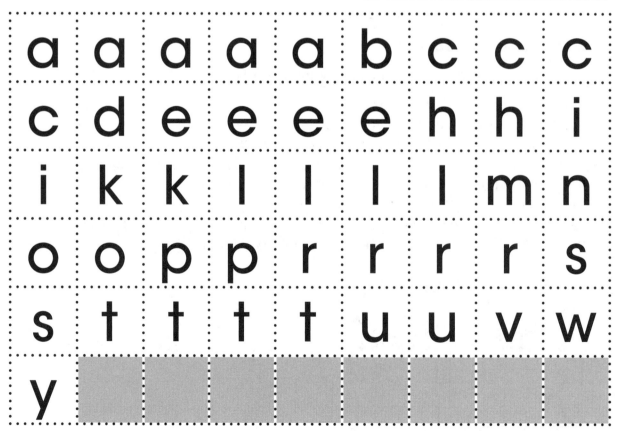

#50682—*Interactive Whiteboards Made Easy: Level 3*   © *Shell Education*

Analogies

Materials

- Level 3 Interactive Whiteboard File (level3.notebook)
- *Understanding Analogies* activity sheet (p. 25)

Interactive Whiteboard Skills

- Advancing pages
- Dragging objects or text

Procedure

1. Launch the Level 3 Notebook file by double-clicking on the icon from the Teacher Resource CD. Press the arrow next to Getting Started activities. Begin this activity by pressing on the Analogies title from the list.

2. Review what an analogy is with the class. Remind students that an analogy is a comparison between two different things in order to find some similarities between them.

3. Press the arrow to **advance** to the first activity page on the interactive whiteboard. Discuss the two words on the left side of the page (*car* and *gas*). Invite students to think of ways these two words are related to one another.

4. Distribute a copy of the *Understanding Analogies* activity sheet (p. 25) to each student. Have students fill in the first analogy frame with the words *car* and *gas*. Now have students focus on the right side of the analogy frame and have them write the word *soil* in their frame.

5. Explain to students that there are three words they need to choose from to finish the analogy frame (*flower*, *sunlight*, or *water*). Once students have chosen and recorded an answer on their activity sheets, invite a student up to the interactive whiteboard to tell which word he or she chose and why. Then, have the student **drag** his or her selection to the empty box to complete the analogy frame. If the student has chosen the correct selection, a check mark will appear. If the student has chosen the incorrect selection, an X will appear.

6. As a class, say the whole analogy together: "*Gas is to car as soil is to flower.*"

7. Press the arrow to **advance** to the next page. Repeat steps 4–6 for the next analogy (*kitten is to cat as seed is to _plant_*).

Analogies *(cont.)*

Procedure *(cont.)*

8. Press the arrow to **advance** to the next page. For this page, the students will need to place all of the terms in the correct place to complete the analogy frame.

9. Have students work with partners to complete this part of the activity. As students complete their frames, have them discuss with their partners the relationships they have found between the terms.

10. Once all of the pairs have completed their frames, invite a pair up to the interactive whiteboard and have them **drag** the terms to fill out the frame. Instruct the pair to explain their reasoning about how the two pairs of terms are related.

11. Press the star to reveal the correct answer to the analogy frame. As a class, say the whole analogy together: *"Arm is to body as leaf is to stem."*

12. Press the arrow to **advance** to the next page. Repeat steps 9–11 for the last analogy (*mail is to postal carrier as pollen is to bee*).

Possible Lesson Ideas

The following lesson suggestions can accompany this getting started activity:

- Read a book about the parts of a plant and their functions. Have students create a flipbook to remember the function of each part of the plant.
- Have students create their own analogies about plants, but have them use pictures rather than words. Instruct them to draw the pictures on four different flashcards and exchange them with other students to solve them.

Interactive Whiteboard File

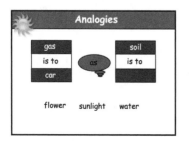
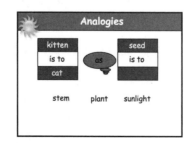
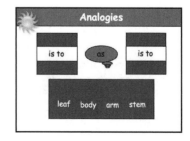

Understanding Analogies

Directions: Follow your teacher's directions to complete the analogies using the boxes below.

1.

is to   as...   is to

2.

is to   as...   is to

3.

is to   as...   is to

4.

is to   as...   is to

Getting Started Activities

Calendar

Materials

- Level 3 Interactive Whiteboard File (level3.notebook)
- *My Day* activity sheet (p. 28)

Interactive Whiteboard Skills

- Advancing pages
- Dragging objects or text
- Using the pen tool

Procedure

1. Launch the Level 3 Notebook file by double-clicking on the icon from the Teacher Resource CD. Press the arrow next to Getting Started activities. Begin this activity by pressing on the Calendar title from the list. *Note:* All of the components of this file are infinitely cloned.

2. Press the arrow to **advance** to the first activity page on the interactive whiteboard. Tell students that they are going to do some short activities to start the day.

3. The first activity is working with the days and date. Invite a student up to the interactive whiteboard and have the student **drag** the correct days into the white boxes on top of the page.

4. Invite a new student up to the board to **drag** the correct day, month, date, and year to the white box in the middle of the page and use the **pen tool** to insert the correct punctuation.

5. Distribute copies of the *My Day* activity page (p. 28) to students. Have them write the correct date on the first line of their activity sheets. Remind them to use correct punctuation.

6. Press the arrow to **advance** to the next page. This activity helps keep track of the weather. Invite a student up to the interactive whiteboard to **drag** the image of the weather that represents the weather outside of the classroom. Once the class agrees on the image of the weather, have the students write at least two sentences on their activity sheets about the weather outside and have them predict what the weather might be tomorrow.

7. Press the arrow to **advance** to the next page. This activity helps keep track of how many days students have been in school so far. Invite a student up to the interactive whiteboard and have the student **drag** the red X onto the present day of school. For example, if it is the first day of school the student will **drag** the X over the "1." The next day, a student will **drag** a second X over the "2."

Calendar *(cont.)*

Procedure *(cont.)*

8. Invite a new student to come up to the interactive whiteboard to represent the day of school by **dragging** the base-ten blocks to the correct columns on the place value chart. (On the tenth day of school, show the students how one tens rod will take the place of 10 individual cubes.) Each day add an X and a blue cube to keep track of the days of school. Have students write at least three sentences on their activity sheets about what they will do today.

9. Press the arrow to **advance** to the next page. This activity helps students work with money. One option is to **drag** coins on top of the piggy bank and ask the class which piggy bank has more money in it.

Another option is to use the **pen tool** to write an amount at the bottom and have a student come up to the interactive whiteboard and **drag** the coins that equal that amount onto the piggy bank. When the activity is complete, have students write a sentence about which strategy they used to add or compare the money.

10. Press the arrow to **advance** to the next page. This activity helps practice fact families. **Drag** two numbers into the white boxes. Invite a student up to the interactive whiteboard to use the **pen tool** to complete the fact family for those two numbers.

11. Have students record the fact family in the last section of their activity sheets.

Possible Lesson Ideas

The following lesson suggestions can accompany this getting started activity:

- Have students write a story problem that can be solved using the fact family studied during the calendar activity.
- Have students keep a learning journal to record things they learn on each day of school. Students record the date and the day of school (25th day, 100th day, etc.) before writing about what they learned.

Interactive Whiteboard File

Name: _____

My Day

Directions: Record details about the calendar activities today according to the directions from your teacher.

Today's Date: _____

Our Weather:

_____

_____

_____

_____

Today's Events:

_____

_____

_____

_____

My Money Problem-Solving Strategy:

_____

_____

_____

_____

Today's Fact Family:

_____ x _____ = _____   _____ ÷ _____ = _____

_____ x _____ = _____   _____ ÷ _____ = _____

Daily Geography

Materials

- Level 3 Interactive Whiteboard File (level3.notebook)
- *Daily Geography* activity sheet (p. 31)

Interactive Whiteboard Skills

- Advancing pages
- Dragging objects or text

Procedure

1. Launch the Level 3 Notebook file by double-clicking on the icon from the Teacher Resource CD. Press the arrow next to Getting Started activities. Begin this activity by pressing on the Daily Geography title from the list.

2. Distribute copies of the *Daily Geography* activity sheet (p. 31) to students.

3. Press the arrow to **advance** to the first activity page on the interactive whiteboard. Allow students to share their observations.

4. Point out the compass rose. Discuss what a compass is and how it is used. Review with the students the four directions that an object or person can travel (*east, west, south, north*).

5. Invite a student to the interactive whiteboard to **drag** the pull tab out from the side. Have the student read the question to the class and follow the directions.

6. In box "1" on their activity sheets, instruct students to draw an arrow to represent the direction in which the boat traveled and then write the word that represents that direction (*arrow should be drawn to the right; east*).

7. Repeat steps 5 and 6 for the remaining pull tabs (*plane: west; car: north; helicopter; south*).

8. Once students have completed those four questions, press the arrow to **advance** to the next page.

9. Tell students that they are going to be asked four questions about bodies of water on the map.

10. Read the question aloud as a class. Tell students that these are multiple-choice questions, so they should record the letter of their choice in the corresponding box on their activity sheets.

Daily Geography *(cont.)*

Procedure *(cont.)*

11. Once all students have recorded their answers, invite a student to the interactive whiteboard and have him or her press the answer he or she chose. If the chosen answer is correct, it will spin. If the chosen answer is not correct, nothing will happen. For Question 1, the answer is "B" (*Pacific Ocean*).

12. Press the arrow to **advance** to the next page to display Question 2.

13. Repeat steps 10–12 to complete the remaining three questions about the bodies of water shown on the maps.

Possible Lesson Ideas

The following lesson suggestions can accompany this getting started activity:

- Have students draw and label maps of the school. Instruct them to create questions about their maps (e.g., *In which direction would I go to get to the library from the playground?*).

- Have students draw maps of their neighborhoods that include their school and home. Then instruct them to write the directions on how to get from their school to home, including cardinal directions.

Interactive Whiteboard File

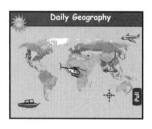 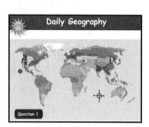 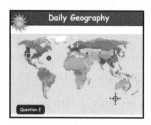

Daily Geography

Directions: Record information in the boxes below according to the directions from your teacher.

1.	2.
3.	4.
1.	2.
3.	4.

Getting Started Activities

Daily Mathematics

Materials

- Level 3 Interactive Whiteboard File (level3.notebook)
- *Math Practice* activity sheet (p. 34)

Procedure

1. Launch the Level 3 Notebook file by double-clicking on the icon from the Teacher Resource CD. Press the arrow next to Getting Started activities. Begin this activity by pressing on the Daily Mathematics title from the list.

2. Tell the class that they are going to do some math review problems. Distribute copies of the *Math Practice* activity sheet (p. 34) to students. Tell students that they are going to place their answers to the problems in the appropriate box on their activity sheets.

3. Divide the class into groups of four. Assign each student in the group a number from 1 to 4.

4. Tell the students that they are going to play a game using the math problems. Press the arrow to **advance** to the first activity page on the interactive whiteboard. Show the class the problems they will be solving.

5. Tell students that they will be told which problem to solve. They may work together to solve the problem, but they must not show their answers until the appropriate time.

Interactive Whiteboard Skills

- Advancing pages
- Dragging objects or text
- Using the spotlight tool

6. To choose which problem to solve, use the **spotlight tool**. Once the **spotlight tool** is activated, you may change its shape. For this activity, the rectangle is most effective. *Note:* The **spotlight tool** may be **dragged** to the floating tool bar to make it easier for the teacher to access.

7. **Drag** the **spotlight tool** over the first problem you want students to solve. Allow them to start solving the problem at the same time. Once every student has an answer written down on his or her activity sheet, select a number between 1 and 4. Those students who were assigned the selected number must display their answers (e.g., if the number 2 was selected, only the students who are assigned number 2 will show their answers). If the student has the correct answer his or her table will receive a point. *Note:* It is possible for multiple groups to receive points.

8. Continue **dragging** the **spotlight tool** until all the problems have been completed. Present the winning team(s) with a reward, if desired.

Daily Mathematics *(cont.)*

Possible Lesson Ideas

The following lesson suggestions can accompany this getting started activity:

- Have students create their own math problems on flash cards. Instruct students to work with partners and exchange cards or have them flip one card over and be the first to solve the problem in order to keep the card.

- Place different math problems around the room and have students stand in front of a problem. Instruct students to solve their problems and record their answers. After one minute, have all the students rotate to a new problem and repeat the procedure. Continue until all the problems are completed.

Interactive Whiteboard File

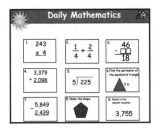

Math Practice

Directions: Record and solve each problem as it is displayed on the interactive whiteboard.

1.	2.	3.
4.	5.	6.
7.	8.	9.

 Alike and Different

Materials

- Level 3 Interactive Whiteboard File (level3.notebook)
- *Alike and Different* activity sheet (p. 37)

Interactive Whiteboard Skills

- Advancing pages
- Using dual page display
- Using the pen tool
- Using the text tool

Procedure

1. Launch the Level 3 Notebook file by double-clicking on the icon from the Teacher Resource CD. Press the arrow next to Vocabulary Development activities. Begin this activity by pressing on the Alike and Different title from the list.

2. Press the arrow to **advance** to the first activity page on the interactive whiteboard. Distribute two copies of the *Alike and Different* activity sheet (p. 37) to students.

3. Read aloud the word pairs in the Alike and Different map (*index* and *appendix*). Invite students who have heard the words before to raise their hands.

4. Choose several students to share what they know about the words. Have students work either individually, in small groups, or as a class to think about how the two words are alike.

5. Invite a student to the interactive whiteboard to use the **pen tool** or the **text tool** to record the ideas in the correct section of the chart. Instruct students to also record the information on their activity sheets.

6. Now have the class think about and discuss how the words are different. Invite a student up to the interactive whiteboard to use the **pen tool** or the **text tool** to record the ideas in the correct section of the chart. Instruct students to also record the information on their activity sheets.

7. Press the arrow to **advance** to the next page and bring up the next Alike and Different map. Students will use their second activity sheets and complete steps 3–6 for the second pair of words (*glossary* and *table of contents*).

8. After the Alike and Different chart is completed, use the **dual page display** to show both charts on the interactive whiteboard. Review both word pairs as a class and talk about how the pairs of words are both alike and different.

Vocabulary Development Activities

 # Alike and Different *(cont.)*

Possible Lesson Ideas

The following lesson suggestions can accompany this vocabulary development activity:

- Individually teach about each part of a nonfiction book. Help students understand the significance of each part of the book and how it is useful to readers. As each part of a book is taught, have students create their own books with all the different parts labeled.

- Use a nonfiction book to teach students about the parts of a book. Then assign the different parts of the book to different table groups and have each table become an "expert" on that part of the book and share with the class.

- Teach a lesson in the library of the school showing how different types of books have different components. Have students go on a scavenger hunt to use the different parts of various books around the library to locate the answers.

Interactive Whiteboard File

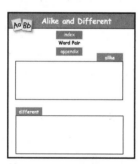 

 # Alike and Different

Directions: Complete the charts below to compare the word pairs. Follow the directions from your teacher.

Word Pair

alike

different

 # Concept of Definition Map

Vocabulary Development Activities

Materials

- Level 3 Interactive Whiteboard File (level3.notebook)
- *Concept of Definition Map* activity sheet (p. 40)

Procedure

1. Launch the Level 3 Notebook file by double-clicking on the icon from the Teacher Resource CD. Press the arrow next to Vocabulary Development activities. Begin this activity by pressing on the Concept of Definition Map title from the list.

2. Press the arrow to **advance** to the first activity page on the interactive whiteboard. Distribute two copies of the *Concept of Definition Map* activity sheet (p. 40) to each student.

3. Read aloud the vocabulary word in the middle of the concept map (*legend*) and have students write the word in the center box on one of their activity sheets. Invite students who have heard the word before to raise their hands.

4. Choose several students who have heard of the word *legend* before to share what they think the word means. If no one in the class has heard of the word before, share with students what the word means (*a story passed down from the past whose truth is accepted by most people but cannot be checked*).

Interactive Whiteboard Skills

- Advancing pages
- Using the pen tool
- Using the text tool

5. As a class, decide on a definition that makes sense to everyone. Invite a student volunteer up to the interactive whiteboard to use the **pen tool** or the **text tool** to write that definition in the "What is it?" box. Instruct students to record that information on their activity sheets, as well.

6. As a class, discuss some things students know about the word *legend*. Use this discussion to create a sentence about what the word is like. Students should come up with ideas that focus on the idea of a story that may or may not be true.

7. Invite a student volunteer up to the interactive whiteboard to use the **pen tool** or the **text tool** to write the sentence in the "What is it like?" box. Instruct students to also record that information on their activity sheets.

8. Have students share examples of the word *legend*. Students may share ideas such as the legend of Paul Bunyon or Black Beard's Ghost.

9. Using the **pen tool**, invite students to draw the examples in the bottom three boxes of the concept map. Instruct students to also draw those examples on their activity sheets.

 # Concept of Definition Map *(cont.)*

Procedure *(cont.)*

10. Press the arrow to **advance** to the next page. Repeat steps 3–5 using the word *ballad (a poem that is usually sung that tells a story of adventure, of romance, or of a hero)*.

11. As a class, discuss some things students know about the word *ballad*. Use this discussion to create a sentence about what the word is like. Students should come up with ideas that focus on the idea of a poem that can be sung.

12. Have a student use the **pen tool** or the **text tool** to write the sentence in the "What is it like?" box. Instruct students to also record that information on their activity sheets.

14. Have students share examples of the word *ballad*. Students may share ideas such as "Yankee Doodle Dandy," "My Darlin' Clementine," or the "Yellow Rose of Texas." Instruct students to record that information on their activity sheets, as well.

15. Using the **pen tool**, invite students to draw the examples in the bottom three boxes of the concept map. Have students draw those examples on their activity sheets, as well.

Possible Lesson Ideas

The following lesson suggestions can accompany this vocabulary development activity:

- Teach a lesson on legends or ballads from a particular time period or country. Then have students create a flipbook illustrating the legend or ballad. Have students work with partners to compare the two legends or ballads.

- Have students work in groups. Each group becomes an expert about a legend or a ballad, then creates *Microsoft PowerPoint*® presentations to explain them.

Interactive Whiteboard File

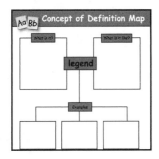 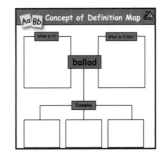

Name:

Concept of Definition Map

Directions: Complete the map according to the directions from your teacher.

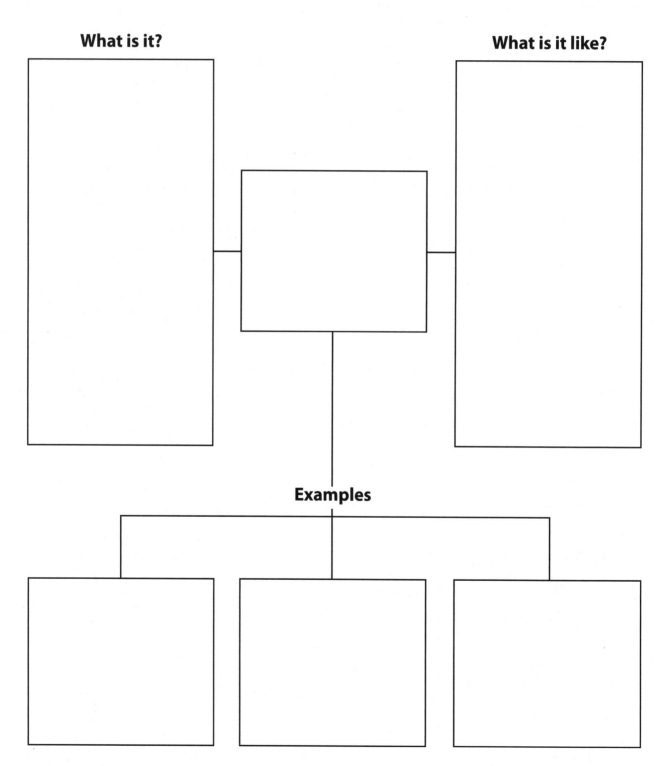

What is it?

What is it like?

Examples

 # Example/Nonexample

Materials

- Level 3 Interactive Whiteboard File (level3.notebook)
- *Example/Nonexample* activity sheet (p. 43)

Procedure

1. Launch the Level 3 Notebook file by double-clicking on the icon from the Teacher Resource CD. Press the arrow next to Vocabulary Development activities. Begin this activity by pressing on the Example/Nonexample title from the list.

2. Press the arrow to **advance** to the first activity page on the interactive whiteboard.

3. Read aloud the term in the middle of the map (*gas*). Invite students who have heard the word before to raise their hands.

4. Choose several students who have heard of the word before to share some examples of the word *gas*. Students can use words, phrases, pictures, or symbols to express their ideas. Allow them to come to the interactive whiteboard and use the **pen tool** or the **text tool** to write their ideas in the "Example" box.

5. Have students look around the room for additional ideas. Invite a student volunteer to the interactive whiteboard to use the **pen tool** or the **text tool** to record the additional examples in the example box.

Interactive Whiteboard Skills

- Advancing pages
- Using the pen tool
- Using the text tool

6. Next, invite students to brainstorm ideas that are nonexamples of a gas. Allow them to come to the interactive whiteboard and use the **pen tool** or the **text tool** to write their ideas in the "Nonexample" box.

7. Press the arrow to **advance** to the next page and bring up the next example/nonexample map. Distribute copies of the *Example/Nonexample* activity sheet (p. 43) to students.

8. Read aloud the term in the middle of the map (*solid*). Invite students who are familiar with the word to raise their hands. Choose several students who are familiar with the word *solid* to share some examples of the word.

9. Read the words at the top of the page. Invite student volunteers to the interactive whiteboard and have them **drag** the words to the appropriate boxes. Discuss how each of the words is either an example or a nonexample of the word *solid*. When a student **drags** a word to a box the student will receive instant feedback about his or her choice. Have students write the words from the interactive whiteboard onto their activity sheets.

 # Example/Nonexample (cont.)

Procedure (cont.)

10. Press the arrow to **advance** to the next page. Read aloud the term in the middle of the map (*liquid*). Invite students who are familiar with the word to raise their hands. Choose students who are familiar with the word *liquid* to share some examples.

11. Look at the pictures at the top of the page. Invite student volunteers to the interactive whiteboard and have them **drag** the pictures to the appropriate boxes. Discuss how each of the words is either an example or a nonexample

of the word *liquid*. When a student **drags** a picture to a box, the student will receive instant feedback to his or her choice. Have students add these words to their activity sheets.

12. Instruct students to work with partners to add their own ideas to their activity sheets. Once students are finished, encourage students to use the **text tool** or the **pen tool** to add a few of their own ideas to the chart.

Possible Lesson Ideas

The following lesson suggestions can accompany this vocabulary development activity:

- Teach a lesson on the changing states of matter. Place an ice cube in a plastic bag for each small group and see who can melt their cube most quickly and discuss why.

- Investigate the water cycle and show how types of matter can change.

- Investigate how molecules move in the three forms of matter. Then have students draw pictures or role play in the front of the room to demonstrate the molecules in all three states.

Interactive Whiteboard File

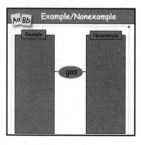 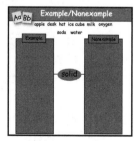 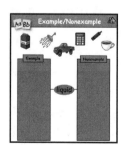

 # Example/Nonexample

Directions: Write the words from the interactive whiteboard in the appropriate boxes below. Then add your own ideas.

Example   **Nonexample**

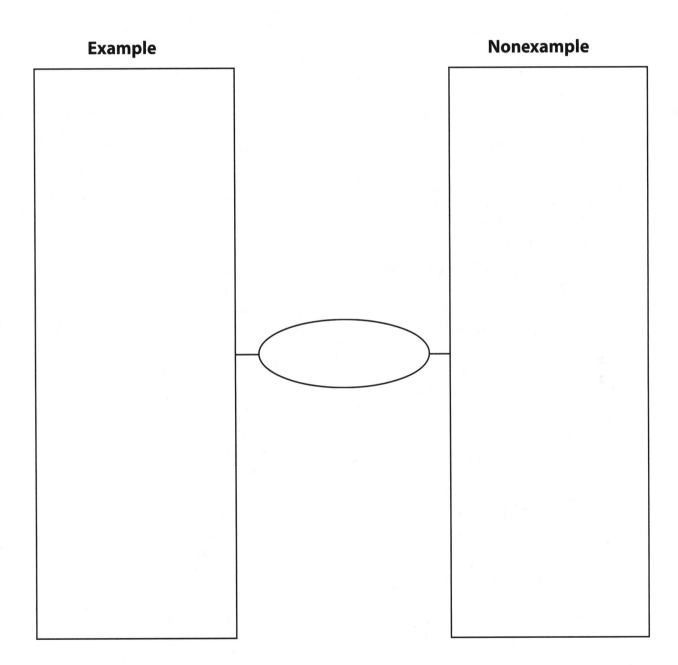

 # Total Physical Response

Materials

- Level 3 Interactive Whiteboard File (level3.notebook)
- *Shape Actions* activity sheet (p. 46)

Procedure

1. Launch the Level 3 Notebook file by double-clicking on the icon from the Teacher Resource CD. Press the arrow next to Vocabulary Development activities. Begin this activity by pressing on the Total Physical Response title from the list.

2. Press the arrow to **advance** to the first activity page on the interactive whiteboard. Distribute copies of the *Shape Actions* activity sheet (p. 46) to students.

3. Press the first **cell shade** located in the "Shape" column and read the word aloud to students (*triangle*).

4. Choose several students who are familiar with the word *triangle* to share what they think the word means. If a student knows how many sides or vertices a *triangle* has, then select the next two **cell shades** to reveal the answers (*3* and *3*).

5. Have students record that information on their activity sheets in the appropriate cells. Then have students draw the shape of the triangle in the correct cell and select the next **cell shade** to show an example of a *triangle*.

Interactive Whiteboard Skills

- Advancing pages
- Using the cell shade
- Using the pen tool
- Using the text tool

6. Discuss the word and call on volunteers who have an idea for a physical action. Give several students an opportunity to share their ideas and have the class decide which physical action they would like to use for the word *triangle*.

7. Invite the student whose suggestion was chosen to the interactive whiteboard to use the **pen tool** or the **text tool** to write his or her name in the box.

8. Press the second **cell shade** in the "Shape" column to reveal the second vocabulary word (*quadrilateral*). Repeat steps 4–7 until the class has a physical response for all five of the vocabulary terms and their activity sheets are completed (*pentagon, hexagon, octagon*).

9. Instruct students to stand and spread out around the room. Call out each term, saying, "Show me _____" (e.g. "Show me <u>triangle</u>").

10. Encourage students to repeat the term chorally as they make the physical response. As they become more familiar with the terms and physical responses, have students close their eyes and then ask for a response.

 # Total Physical Response *(cont.)*

Procedure *(cont.)*

11. Press the arrow to **advance** to the next page. Invite a student volunteer up to the interactive whiteboard and press on the die. Have students either individually, in small groups, or as a whole class, create the physical response that corresponds to the term that is rolled. Students should chorally say the word as they make the response.

12. Continue having students press the die until all of the terms have been rolled at least once.

Possible Lesson Ideas

The following lesson suggestions can accompany this vocabulary development activity:

- Create a list of real life objects corresponding to the different shapes. Have students go on a school scavenger hunt for the shapes and use digital cameras to take pictures of the shapes they find and their locations.

- Teach a lesson about the different types of quadrilaterals (*square*, *rectangle*, *rhombus*), and have students create posters to demonstrate the differences among them.

- Investigate the shapes that are made when multiple shapes are put together (e.g., *a square and a triangle*). Have students use paper shapes to create new designs using the shapes investigated in the vocabulary activity.

Interactive Whiteboard File

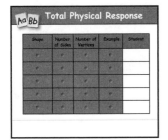 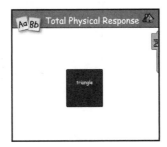

Vocabulary Development Activities

 # Shape Actions

Directions: Draw the actions chosen for each of the vocabulary words listed below.

Shape	Number of Sides	Number of Vertices	Example	Action
triangle				
quadrilateral				
pentagon				
hexagon				
octagon				

 # Word Tiles

Materials

- Level 3 Interactive Whiteboard File (level3.notebook)
- *Understanding Prefixes* activity sheet (p. 49)

Interactive Whiteboard Skills

- Advancing pages
- Dragging objects or text

Procedure

1. Launch the Level 3 Notebook file by double-clicking on the icon from the Teacher Resource CD. Press the arrow next to Vocabulary Development activities. Begin this activity by pressing on the Word Tiles title from the list. *Note:* All of the word tiles are infinitely cloned so that students can see how root words can change based on their prefixes.

2. Press the arrow to **advance** to the first activity page on the interactive whiteboard. Distribute copies of the *Understanding Prefixes* activity sheet (p. 49) to students.

3. Tell the class that they are going to focus on learning and applying the four prefixes displayed (*re-, un-, dis-, mis-*). Invite a student to the board to **drag** the first pull tab and move it down the board in line with the first prefix "re-." Review the meaning of the prefix (*again*).

4. To help students see how a prefix can change the meaning of a word, **drag** a clone of the word tile prefix "re-" into the space below it. Also **drag** a clone of the word tile "do" from the bottom of the page, and place it next to the "re-" word tile. Discuss with the class what the word *do* means, then discuss with the class what the word *redo* means.

5. Have students record the meaning of the prefix *re-* and the provided example (*redo*) on their activity sheets.

6. As a class, try making other words with the prefix *re-* using the word tiles. Have students add the new words to their activity sheets (possible words: *replay, rewrite, reappear, reapprove*).

7. Repeat steps 3–6 for the remaining prefixes (possible words: *un-: unclog, unable, unlucky, undo; dis-: dishonest, disapprove, disappear, disable; mis-: mismatch, misjudge, misspell, misplay*).

8. Press the arrow to **advance** to the next page. Tell students that they are going to be shown an incomplete sentence and that it needs a word with one of the four prefixes added to complete it.

9. **Drag** the pull tab to the left to reveal the sentence to the class. Invite a student to the interactive whiteboard and read the sentence to the class.

Vocabulary Development Activities

 # Word Tiles *(cont.)*

Procedure *(cont.)*

10. Tell the class that one of the prefixes needs to be added to the root word, *move* to make the sentence correct. Have the students discuss with partners what they think is the correct answer. Invite students to share their answers with the class.

11. Have the student at the board **drag** the correct prefix to the front of the root word. As a class, read the sentence aloud to check that the correct prefix was chosen (*re-*). Have students write the correct word on their activity sheets.

12. Press the arrow to **advance** to the next page. Continue steps 10 and 11 for the remaining sentences (*mis-*; *un-*; *dis-*).

Possible Lesson Ideas

The following lesson suggestions can accompany this vocabulary development activity:

• Give each student four sticky notes. Have students write a prefix on each of the sticky notes. On 3" × 5" cards, write root words that students are familiar with. Have students place the sticky notes in front of the root word to see if they have made a new word. If they do, have them write a sentence using the new word.

• Invite three or four students to the front of the room and have each student represent a different prefix. Select another student to represent a root word. Provide students with signs displaying either the root word or prefix they represent. Have students who are prefixes come and stand next to the root word to see how many new words can be made.

Interactive Whiteboard File

  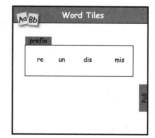

 # Understanding Prefixes

Directions: Complete the map below using the directions from your teacher.
Then, on the lines below, write the correct word to complete the sentences shown
on the interactive whiteboard.

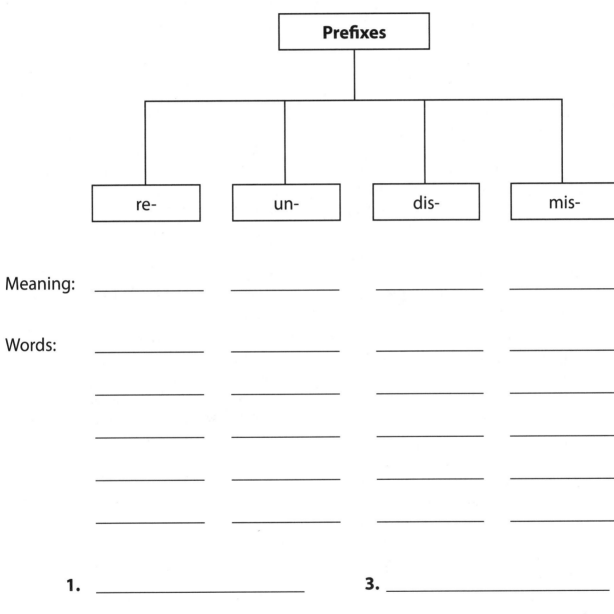

Meaning: _____ _____ _____ _____

Words: _____ _____ _____ _____

1. _____   3. _____

2. _____   4. _____

Analyze the Picture

Materials

- Level 3 Interactive Whiteboard File (level3.notebook)
- *Analyze This!* activity sheet (p. 52)

Interactive Whiteboard Skills

- Advancing pages
- Dragging objects or text

Procedure

1. Launch the Level 3 Notebook file by double-clicking on the icon from the Teacher Resource CD. Press the arrow next to Activating Prior Knowledge activities. Begin this activity by pressing on the Analyze the Picture title from the list.

2. Press the arrow to **advance** to the first activity page on the interactive whiteboard. Distribute copies of the *Analyze This!* activity sheet (p. 52) to the students.

3. Tell the class that they are going to observe two pictures that relate to something that will be studied in class.

4. **Drag** "Pull Tab 1" to the right to reveal a question for the class to answer (*What do you observe in the picture?*). Have students share their observations and predictions with the class. Then, in the section labeled "1" on their activity sheets, have students list any observations or predictions about the two pictures. Encourage students to use adjectives to describe their observations.

5. Repeat steps 4 and 5 with the remaining pull tabs. Students will respond to each of the questions on their activity sheets.

6. On the lines provided at the bottom of the activity sheets, have students make predictions about what they think they will be studying. Encourage students to use adjectives to describe the topic of study and what they think they will be learning.

7. Once the class has made their predictions and observations, press the arrow to **advance** to the next page.

8. Read the background information to students about the Carlisle school. Have a discussion about the observations they made about the picture and the information they just received from the background information.

Activating Prior Knowledge Activities

Analyze the Picture *(cont.)*

Possible Lesson Ideas

The following lesson suggestions can accompany this activating prior knowledge activity:

- Have students write a descriptive, fictional story regarding what the picture is about.
- Teach about current American Indian culture and how Native Americans were treated in the United States during the 20th century.

Interactive Whiteboard File

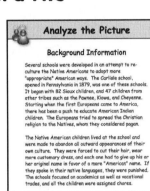

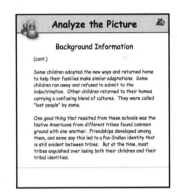

Name: _____

Analyze This!

Directions: Write words or phrases in the boxes below based on what you see in the image displayed on the interactive whiteboard. Use adjectives in your writing.

1.	**2.**
3.	**4.**

Directions: Make predictions about what you think you will be studying next.

_____

_____

_____

_____

_____

_____

_____

Anticipation Guide

Materials

- Level 3 Interactive Whiteboard File (level3.notebook)
- *Anticipation Guide* activity sheet (p. 55)
- class set of *Charlotte's Web* by E. B. White (1980)

Interactive Whiteboard Skills

- Advancing pages
- Dragging objects or text
- Using the pen tool

Procedure

1. Launch the Level 3 Notebook file by double-clicking on the icon from the Teacher Resource CD. Press the arrow next to Activating Prior Knowledge activities. Begin this activity by pressing on the Anticipation Guide title from the list.

2. Press the arrow to **advance** to the first activity page on the interactive whiteboard. Distribute copies of the *Anticipation Guide* activity sheet (p. 55) to students.

3. Tell the class that before they read their next story, they are going to do some previewing to make predictions about the story *Charlotte's Web*. Tell students that previewing is a comprehension strategy that helps them set a purpose for reading and helps them predict what the story may be about.

4. Before showing students the statements they will be analyzing, have them work with partners to perform a picture/title walk. Have students look at the pictures as well as the titles of each chapter to help gain insight into the story.

5. After the picture/title walk, **drag** the first pull tab to the left to reveal the first statement. Have students write this statement on their activity sheets.

6. Either as a class or individually, have students decide if they agree or disagree with that statement based on their picture/title walk. Invite a student up to the interactive whiteboard and **drag** either the word *Agree* or *Disagree* from the heading to the appropriate box, depending on whether he or she agrees or disagrees with the statement. Discuss the choice as a class.

7. Repeat steps 5 and 6 with the next three pull tabs. Remind students that as they read the book they will find out whether they are correct. This gives students a purpose for reading.

Activating Prior Knowledge Activities

Anticipation Guide *(cont.)*

Procedure *(cont.)*

8. After reading the book, discuss the statements on the pull tabs. Either with partners or as a whole class, have students look for the pages in the book that prove or disprove the statements. When useful evidence is found, invite a student up to the interactive whiteboard to use the **pen tool** and record the page number of the evidence in the appropriate box.

9. If the class correctly predicts a statement, have a student come up to the interactive whiteboard and **drag** the green check mark to the fourth column box to show that the class's prediction was correct. If the class was incorrect, have the student drag the red X to the white square. Both the check mark and the X are infinitely cloned.

Possible Lesson Ideas

The following lesson suggestions can accompany this activating prior knowledge activity:

- Place the students in small groups and have them act out their predictions rather than just writing them down. After reading the story, have the groups revise their skits, if needed.

- Have the students read a short story on their own and create anticipation guides for another student. Have partners trade anticipation guides and short stories to complete and read independently.

Interactive Whiteboard File

Activating Prior Knowledge Activities

Anticipation Guide

Directions: Write the statements shown on the interactive whiteboard in the appropriate boxes. Check whether you agree or disagree in the second column of the chart. Complete the rest of the chart after reading the book.

Statement	Agree or Disagree	Page	Correct (✓) or Incorrect (✗)

Activating Prior Knowledge Activities

Historical Document

Materials

- Level 3 Interactive Whiteboard File (level3.notebook)
- *Stay in School* activity sheet (p. 58)

Interactive Whiteboard Skills

- Advancing pages
- Dragging objects or text
- Using the spotlight tool

Procedure

1. Launch the Level 3 Notebook file by double-clicking on the icon from the Teacher Resource CD. Press the arrow next to Activating Prior Knowledge activities. Begin this activity by pressing on the Historical Document title from the list.

2. Press the arrow to **advance** to the first activity page on the interactive whiteboard and distribute copies of the *Stay in School* activity sheet (p. 58) to students.

3. Tell the class that they are going to review a document from the year 1917. Ask students what they see in the document. Have them record their observations on their activity sheets.

4. Based on their observations, ask students what they think this document is showing (*a graph of a worker's income based on his level of school*).

5. Use the **spotlight tool** to point out specific parts of the graph that will help students understand the information in the document more thoroughly. From the "View" dropdown menu, click on "Zoom" to increase the size of the picture.

6. Before asking specific questions about reading the bar graph, ask the class if they can make any statements using the data on the graph. After the students have shared some of their thoughts, **drag** "Pull Tab 1" out to display the question to the class. Have the students answer the question in a complete sentence on their papers.

7. Discuss the answer to the problem as a class. Then **drag** "Pull Tab 1" back to the side of the page and **drag** "Pull Tab 2" out. Students should also respond to this question on their activity sheets.

8. Repeat step 6 until all four questions have been discussed.

9. After the students have finished answering all four questions, place them in small groups and have the groups work together to brainstorm more questions that can be used to analyze the graph.

Activating Prior Knowledge Activities

Historical Document *(cont.)*

Possible Lesson Ideas

The following lesson suggestions can accompany this activating prior knowledge activity:

- Discuss with the class how they can take the data in a bar graph and turn it into a line graph. Place students in small groups and give each group the same data but assign each group a different way they must display the data.

- Place the students in small groups and have them come up with a question they would like to ask the class, grade level, or school. Have them gather the data to the question and create their own bar graph to show their results.

- Have students search their community for other real-world examples of graphs. Students can search places such as newspapers, magazines, the Internet, travel brochures, and advertisements.

Interactive Whiteboard File

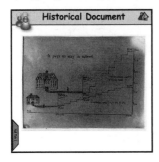

Stay in School

Directions: Look at the document on the interactive whiteboard and respond to the questions below.

Write your observations on the lines below.

_____

_____

_____

_____

_____

1. At 25 years old, how much more money per week did the worker make who stayed in school until age 18?

_____

_____

2. Which person earns more money according to the results in the graph?

_____

_____

3. What point is the author of this graph trying to make? Why?

_____

_____

_____

4. How is math used to help the author prove his or her point?

_____

_____

_____

_____

Activating Prior Knowledge Activities

List, Group, Label

Materials

- Level 3 Interactive Whiteboard File (level3.notebook)
- *Water, Anyone?* activity sheet (p. 61)
- sticky notes

Procedure

1. Launch the Level 3 Notebook file by double-clicking on the icon from the Teacher Resource CD. Press the arrow next to Activating Prior Knowledge activities. Begin this activity by pressing on the List, Group, Label title from the list.

2. Press the arrow to **advance** to the first activity page on the interactive whiteboard and distribute copies of the *Water, Anyone?* activity sheet (p. 61) to students.

3. Ask student volunteers to read aloud the terms provided in the box at the top of the first activity page. Discuss the terms as a class and make sure that students know the meanings of all of the terms displayed.

4. Divide the class into groups of two to four students. Provide each group with sticky notes and have them copy the terms onto the sticky notes (one term per sticky note).

5. Allow groups time to organize the terms into different categories. Have students work on a desk so they can easily move the sticky notes into the categories chosen. Explain to groups that all the terms must somehow be included. Students must also record their work on their activity sheets.

Interactive Whiteboard Skills

- Advancing pages
- Dragging objects or text
- Using the text tool

6. After the class has placed the sticky notes into categories, select a group to come up to the interactive whiteboard. Then, allow the group to **drag** the terms into the green boxes under the labels. The group should be able to justify why it chose to place each term into the various categories. After the group has moved all of the words, have the class try to guess the names of the groups' categories. After several suggestions have been made, have the group use the **text tool** to write category names they chose on the interactive whiteboard.

7. Invite a second group to share its ideas using the same procedures as in step 6.

8. Discuss as a class why it is possible to have different categories and still have "correct" answers. Students should begin to see that words could be related differently depending on the categories chosen.

9. Press the arrow to **advance** to the next page. Explain to students that this represents another way that the words can be grouped.

Activating Prior Knowledge Activities

List, Group, Label *(cont.)*

Possible Lesson Ideas

The following lesson suggestions can accompany this activating prior knowledge activity:

- Investigate the air in the water by taking a mirror and placing it above boiling water. Have students write down what they observe and ask students if there is water in the air.

- Get four glasses. Place one in a freezer, fill one with ice, place one in the refrigerator, and use one glass just as a control. After 10 minutes, line up all four glasses and have students write down what they have observed.

- Place some salt water in a shallow lid. Let the water sit for at least one day on a sunny windowsill. Then have students observe what is in the lid now and discuss what happened to the water.

Interactive Whiteboard File

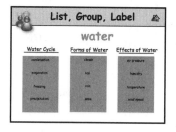

Name:

Water, Anyone?

Directions: Look at the words in the box below. Group the words by how they are related. Then create labels for the categories. Record your ideas in the spaces provided.

water		
air pressure	freezing	rain
clouds	hail	snow
condensation	humidity	temperature
evaporation	precipitation	wind speed

Picture Predictions

Materials

- Level 3 Interactive Whiteboard File (level3.notebook)
- *Adjective Predictions* activity sheet (p. 64)

Interactive Whiteboard Skills

- Advancing pages
- Dragging objects or text
- Using the pen tool
- Using the text tool

Procedure

1. Launch the Level 3 Notebook file by double-clicking on the icon from the Teacher Resource CD. Press the arrow next to Activating Prior Knowledge activities. Begin this activity by pressing on the Picture Predictions title from the list.

2. Press the arrow to **advance** to the first activity page on the interactive whiteboard and distribute two copies of the *Adjective Predictions* activity sheet (p. 64) to students.

3. Tell the class they are going to observe three pictures. As the pictures are revealed, students will come up with adjectives that can describe each picture.

4. Have students work with partners or in small groups. Reveal the first picture by pressing on the "1." (*pencil*) In their groups, allow students one minute to list as many adjectives as they can about the pencil in the space provided on their activity sheets.

5. After one minute, have students share some of the adjectives they listed. Record students' adjectives in the box labeled "Adjectives" using the **text tool** or the **pen tool**.

6. Repeat steps 4 and 5 for the pictures labeled "2." and "3."

7. Now have the students write predictions about what all three images have in common. **Drag** the pull tab out to reveal a possible prediction sentence.

8. Press the arrow to **advance** to the next page. Repeat steps 4–7 on this page and see if students can come up with a prediction based on the commonalities of the next three pictures. Students will need a second copy of the *Adjective Predictions* activity sheet (p. 64) in order to complete this part of the activity.

Picture Predictions *(cont.)*

Possible Lesson Ideas

The following lesson suggestions can accompany this activating prior knowledge activity:

- Pass out a piece of paper with every letter of the alphabet on it, along with a little space next to each letter. Have students come up with adjectives describing themselves. Each adjective must start with a different letter of the alphabet.
- Have students select an object in the room and have them write a paragraph using descriptive adjectives describing it. Do not have students write what the object is or tell his or her classmates. As the student reads his or her paragraph out loud, the other students will try to draw the object only by listening to the description.

Interactive Whiteboard File

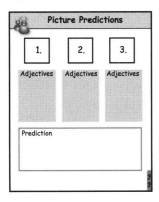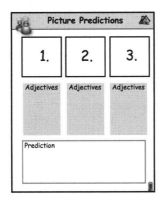

Activating Prior Knowledge Activities

Name:

Adjective Predictions

Directions: Look at the images displayed. Write as many adjectives as you can to describe the images. Then, write a prediction about what the three objects have in common.

Adjectives	**Adjectives**	**Adjectives**

Prediction

Venn Diagram

Materials

- Level 3 Interactive Whiteboard File (level3.notebook)
- *Comparing Sports* activity sheet (p. 67)
- sheet of paper

Interactive Whiteboard Skills

- Advancing pages
- Dragging objects or text
- Using the pen tool
- Using the text tool

Procedure

1. Launch the Level 3 Notebook file by double-clicking on the icon from the Teacher Resource CD. Press the arrow next to Graphic Organizer activities. Begin this activity by pressing on the Venn Diagram title from the list.

2. Press the arrow to **advance** to the first activity page on the interactive whiteboard and distribute copies of the *Comparing Sports* activity sheet (p. 67) to students.

3. Tell the class that they are going to write a paragraph comparing soccer and baseball. (Make this assignment more challenging by having students write two paragraphs.) Students will find traits that both sports have in common as well as traits that only pertain to each sport.

4. Tell students that before they start writing, they must first organize their thoughts and ideas onto a graphic organizer (Venn diagram). This step of the writing process is known as prewriting.

5. Select a student to come up to the interactive whiteboard and use the **pen tool** or the **text tool** to write the word *soccer* at the top of the circle on the left and the word *baseball* at the top of the circle on the right. Have the rest of the class fill out their own Venn diagrams.

6. As a class, discuss the sections of the Venn diagram and ask students what type of information belongs in each section. Make sure students clearly understand that the common traits of soccer and baseball will go in the middle section.

7. As a class, read the words and phrases found below the Venn diagram. Make sure students understand the meaning of each word or phrase.

8. Invite a student up to the interactive whiteboard and have him or her **drag** the traits that both sports have in common into the middle section. Discuss with the class why these traits belong in the middle section (*sprint, uses a round ball, played outside, wear cleats*). Have students record these traits on their activity sheets.

Venn Diagram *(cont.)*

Procedure *(cont.)*

9. Invite another student up to the interactive whiteboard and have him or her **drag** the traits that only pertain to soccer into the section on the left. Discuss with the class why these traits belong in that section (*goalie, goals, rectangular field, two halves*). Have students record these traits on their activity sheets.

10. Invite another student up to the interactive whiteboard and have him or her **drag** the traits that only pertain to baseball into the section on the right. Discuss with the class why these traits belong in that section (*home run, diamond field, nine innings, use gloves*). Have students record these traits on their activity sheets.

11. Once the Venn diagrams are completed, have students begin to write their paragraph(s) on their own papers. Inform the class they should begin with the traits that are different for each sport. Tell students that each trait can be used as an idea for a sentence.

12. As students write, remind them to refer back to their Venn diagrams in order to keep themselves organized and remember all of the traits.

Possible Lesson Ideas

The following lesson suggestions can accompany this graphic organizer activity:

- Once students' paragraphs are complete, have them switch with partners and work at editing/revising their work.
- After learning two different algorithms for addition, multiplication, subtraction, or division, have students compare and contrast the procedures using a Venn diagram.
- After reading a story, use the Venn diagram to compare and contrast two characters from the story.

Interactive Whiteboard File

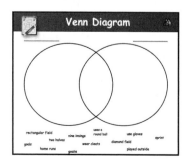

Name:

Comparing Sports

Directions: Write words to compare two items as instructed by your teacher.

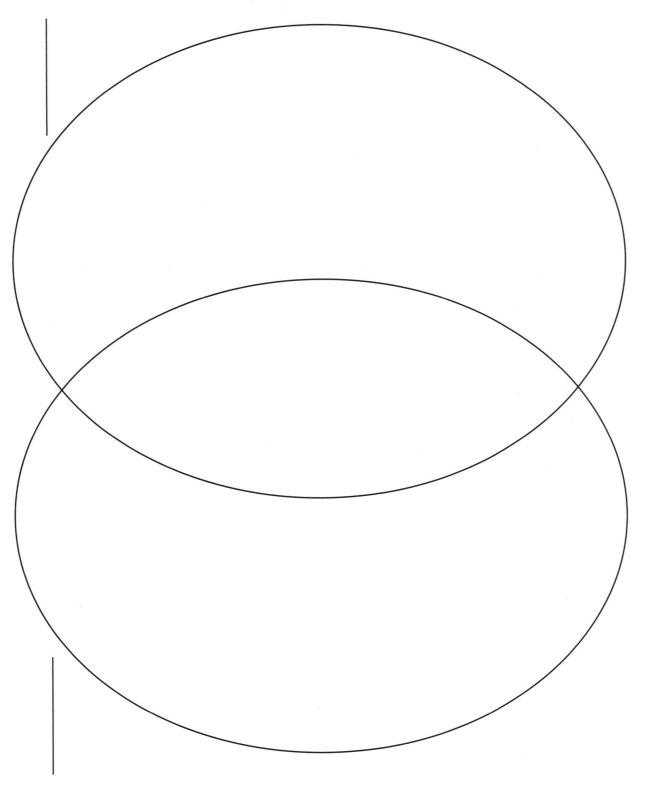

Flow Chart

Graphic Organizer Activities

Materials

- Level 3 Interactive Whiteboard File (level3.notebook)
- *How to Make…* activity sheet (p. 70)

Interactive Whiteboard Skills

- Advancing pages
- Dragging objects or text

Procedure

1. Launch the Level 3 Notebook file by double-clicking on the icon from the Teacher Resource CD. Press the arrow next to Graphic Organizer activities. Begin this activity by pressing on the Flow Chart title from the list.

2. Press the arrow to **advance** to the first activity page on the interactive whiteboard and distribute copies of the *How to Make…* activity sheet (p. 70) to students.

3. Tell students that today they are going to create a set of written instructions about the sequential steps to make a peanut butter and jelly sandwich.

4. Explain that a flow chart is a step-by-step illustration of a specific event. Tell the class that you are first going to arrange sentences in the correct sequence using the flow chart. Invite a student up to the interactive whiteboard to **drag** the red star to the right to see the first sentence. Discuss with the class where it might go in the flow chart. Tell the class that they can move the sentence later if they think it needs to be adjusted.

5. Once the class has decided where the first sentence should go, have the student **drag** the sentence to the appropriate box.

6. Repeat steps 4 and 5 until all of the sentences are placed on the flow chart.

7. Have students work with partners to determine the correct sequential steps to making a peanut butter and jelly sandwich.

8. Once all sentences are placed, have students record all of the sentences on their activity sheets. If necessary, allow students to draw images to help them remember the contents of the text.

Flow Chart *(cont.)*

Possible Lesson Ideas

The following lesson suggestions can accompany this graphic organizer activity:

- Have students create their own flow charts about their favorite sandwich or on another type of food they know how to make. Then have students create an explanatory piece of writing that details the information included in their flow charts.

- Have each student select five major points in his or her life (e.g., *being born, the first day of school*) and place them on a time line.

- Find two recipes that show how to create the same item and have the students create flow charts for each recipe. Then have students compare and contrast the two recipes to see which one is "better."

- Bring in a popular board game and have students write the directions using a flow chart on how to play the game for a first-time user.

Interactive Whiteboard File

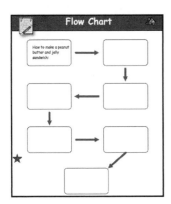

How to Make...

Directions: Complete the flow chart according to the directions from your teacher.

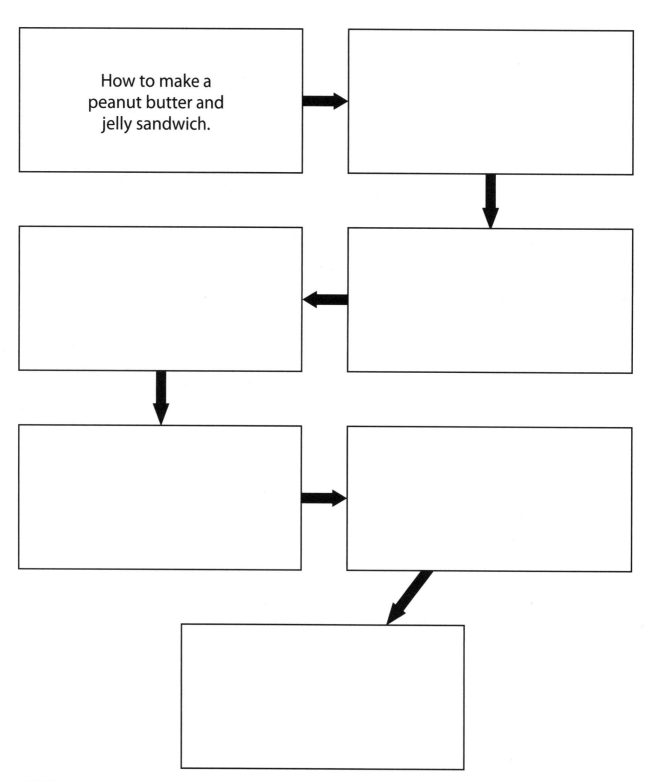

How to make a
peanut butter and
jelly sandwich.

Graphic Organizer Activities

KWL Chart

Materials

- Level 3 Interactive Whiteboard File (level3.notebook)
- *My KWL* activity sheet (p. 73)
- sheet of paper

Interactive Whiteboard Skills

- Advancing pages
- Using the pen tool
- Using the screen shade
- Using the text tool

Procedure

1. Launch the Level 3 Notebook file by double-clicking on the icon from the Teacher Resource CD. Press the arrow next to Graphic Organizer activities. Begin this activity by pressing on the KWL Chart title from the list.

2. Press the arrow to **advance** to the first activity page on the interactive whiteboard and distribute copies of the *My KWL* activity sheet (p. 73) to students. Slide the **screen shade** down to show the KWL title and the topic "The Sun."

3. Tell the class they are going to learn about the sun using a KWL chart. Inform the class that a KWL chart helps us organize information. It helps us determine our prior knowledge, what we already know, about the sun.

4. Ask the class if they know what the initials stand for in KWL. Review each initial with the class explaining that the "K" stands for what we *k*now about the sun. The "W" stands for what we *w*ant to learn and the "L" stands for what we *l*earned.

5. Slide the **screen shade** down until the first box is revealed to the class. ("What do I **K**now?"). Ask the class to brainstorm about the sun. Use the **pen tool** to record the students' suggestions about what they know about the sun in the first box. Do not be concerned if the statement is true or not. (An option is to place the student's name next to each suggestion to give it ownership.) Have the students fill out their activity sheets as you record information on the interactive whiteboard. ***Tip:*** To control the management of all students wanting to share out, use a soft ball or stuffed animal. Only the student who has possession of the object can share out.

6. Now slide the **screen shade** down until the middle box is revealed to the class. (What do I **W**ant to know?"). Ask the class to think of questions they might want to learn about the sun. Again, putting names next to student suggestions is an option.

KWL Chart *(cont.)*

Procedure *(cont.)*

7. After you have listed the questions on the board and students have filled in their charts, ask the class what resources can be used to help find out the answers to these questions. Use the **pen tool** to record the resources suggested by students on a separate sheet of paper. Some examples might be a book, the Internet, videos, or a magazine.

8. Using one or more of the resources listed, try to answer some of the questions the students have posed for the class. Once an answer has been found, slide the **screen shade** all the way down to reveal the last box (the "L" box) for the class. Tell students that the last box is for the answers that they have found to their questions.

9. You can assign individual students or groups of students particular questions and let them use the resources to find the answers and share out their results. You might also tell the class that as they continue to study the sun in this unit they will fill in the last box as they find the answers.

Possible Lesson Ideas

The following lesson suggestions can accompany this graphic organizer activity:

- Create a sundial using clay and a craft stick. Take the sundials out at different times of the day to tell the time. Students can use chalk to create a clock around their sundial.

- Have students outline each other's shadows using chalk outside in the morning and again in the afternoon. Have students measure the distance the shadow has moved from the beginning of the day to the end of the day.

- On a flashcard, have students write three truths and one myth about the sun. Have students read cards out loud and see if the class can identify the myth.

Interactive Whiteboard File

Name:

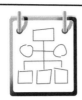

My KWL

Directions: Record the information from the interactive whiteboard onto your KWL chart below.

The Sun

What do I *K*now?

What do I *W*ant to know?

What have I *L*earned?

T-Chart

Materials

- Level 3 Interactive Whiteboard File (level3.notebook)
- *Representing Numbers* activity sheet (p. 76)

Interactive Whiteboard Skills

- Advancing pages
- Dragging objects or text
- Using the pen tool

Procedure

1. Launch the Level 3 Notebook file by double-clicking on the icon from the Teacher Resource CD. Press the arrow next to Graphic Organizer activities. Begin this activity by pressing on the T-Chart title from the list.

2. Press the arrow to **advance** to the first activity page on the interactive whiteboard and distribute copies of the *Representing Numbers* activity sheet (p. 76) to students.

3. Tell the class that today they are going to use what they know about place value to represent different numbers. As a class, discuss the information provided on the T-chart. Make sure students understand what the terms *Numeral, Expanded Form*, and *Base-Ten Blocks* mean.

4. Tell the class that the T-chart will help keep the information organized. Press the purple hexagon to reveal the first number. As a class, say the number aloud (*452*).

5. Select a student to come up to the interactive whiteboard and **drag** the correct amount of base-ten blocks to represent the number. *Note:* The blocks are infinitely cloned so the student can **drag** as many blocks as needed (*4 hundred blocks, 5 tens rods, and 2 unit cubes*).

6. As a class, check the student's work and then have students draw the corresponding base-ten blocks on their activity sheets.

7. Ask a new student to come to the interactive whiteboard and use the **pen tool** to write the number in expanded form. Discuss how the base-ten blocks and the expanded form look very similar (*400 + 50 + 2*). Have students record the number in expanded form on their activity sheets, as well.

8. Repeat steps 4–7 for the remaining numbers on the chart. At the bottom of their pages, have students write at least two sentences to explain how knowing about place value helps them represent these numbers in three different ways.

T-Chart *(cont.)*

Possible Lesson Ideas

The following lesson suggestions can accompany this graphic organizer activity:

- Have students add a column to their charts and come up with a third way to represent the numbers from the activity. Encourage students to use their knowledge of place value in the representation they choose.

- Have students work with partners and provide each pair with an empty place value chart and dice. Have them roll the dice and place that number in their chart with the goal of trying to create the largest number.

- Use this activity as a review of place value before introducing the ten thousands and hundred thousands places to students.

Interactive Whiteboard File

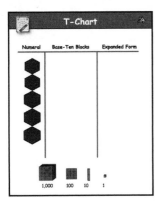

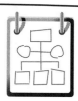

Representing Numbers

Directions: Write the numerals from the interactive whiteboard in the first column. Use the T-chart to record two other representations of that number.

Numeral	Base-Ten Blocks	Expanded Form

Directions: Write two sentences to explain how numerals can be represented in different ways.

_____

_____

_____

Web Map

Materials

- Level 3 Interactive Whiteboard File (level3.notebook)
- *Landform Web* activity sheet (p. 79)

Interactive Whiteboard Skills

- Advancing pages
- Dragging objects or text
- Using dual page display *(optional)*
- Using the pen tool
- Using the text tool

Procedure

1. Launch the Level 3 Notebook file by double-clicking on the icon from the Teacher Resource CD. Press the arrow next to Graphic Organizer activities. Begin this activity by pressing on the Web Map title from the list.

2. Press the arrow to **advance** to the first activity page on the interactive whiteboard and distribute several copies of the *Landform Web* activity sheet (p. 79) to students.

3. Tell the class that they are going to learn about different types of brainstorming to see what they already know about landforms and make connections between them.

4. Have students write the word *landform* in the bubble on their activity sheets. **Drag** the pull tab out to reveal pictures of different types of landforms.

5. After revealing the first picture, ask the class if anyone can identify the landform. Invite a student to the interactive whiteboard to use the **pen tool** or **text tool** to write the word *ocean* in one of the white circles. Have students also add this to their

activity sheets. Continue **dragging** the pull tab out to reveal another picture until all the circles are filled in *(ocean, lake, mountain, river, and valley)*.

6. Press the arrow to **advance** to the next page and tell students to use a new activity sheet. Ask the class to brainstorm about *the ocean*. The students may describe the characteristics, give specific examples, compare it to something else, or share out anything else they might know about the ocean. Use the **pen tool** or the **text tool** to record students' ideas. Also have students add these ideas to their activity sheets.

7. Repeat step 6 until students have brainstormed about each landform.

8. Have students share connections between the landforms. Encourage them to observe similarities or differences between the landforms. Use the **dual page display** to compare two landform webs together on the interactive whiteboard.

Web Map *(cont.)*

Possible Lesson Ideas

The following lesson suggestions can accompany this graphic organizer activity:

- Have students create a matching game by drawing the different landforms on 3"× 5" cards. On another set of 3"× 5" cards have them write the names of the landform and play against a partner.

- Read different "clues" about a particular landform and see if students can infer which landform the teacher is describing. Start with general clues and gradually have them get more specific.

- Give a picture of a landform to each student. Tell students to pretend they are on vacation at that landform and they need to write postcards to their friends describing their landform and what they are doing.

Interactive Whiteboard File

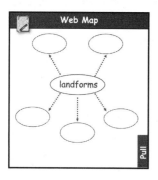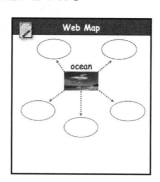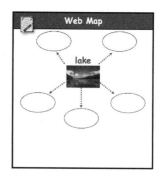

Landform Web

Directions: Use the information on the interactive whiteboard to create a web map about landforms.

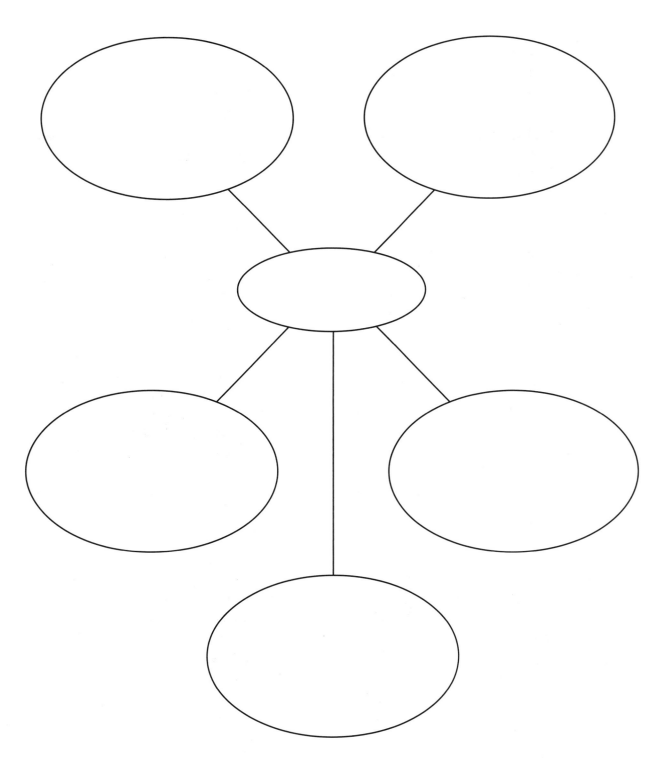

Cause and Effect

Materials

- Level 3 Interactive Whiteboard File (level3.notebook)
- *Causes and Effects* activity sheet (p. 82)

Interactive Whiteboard Skills

- Advancing pages
- Dragging objects or text

Procedure

1. Launch the Level 3 Notebook file by double-clicking on the icon from the Teacher Resource CD. Press the arrow next to Comprehension activities. Begin this activity by pressing on the Cause and Effect title from the list.

2. Before the lesson starts, untie your shoe or place an object on the floor. Press the arrow to **advance** to the first activity page on the interactive whiteboard and distribute copies of the *Causes and Effects* activity sheet (p. 82) to students. As you distribute the activity sheets, intentionally trip over your shoe laces or the object. This will get the students' attention. Discuss with the class what happened and why it happened.

3. Tell the class when something happens there is always a cause and effect. A cause is what makes something happen. To find the cause, you need to ask yourself, "What happened first?" The shoe laces becoming untied or the object left on the floor is the cause.

4. Now ask the class what happened because the shoe lace was untied or the object was left on the floor (*you tripped*). Explain that an effect is what happens because of something else (the cause). To find the effect, you need to ask yourself, "What happened second?"

5. Direct students' attention to the interactive whiteboard and read the first cause to the class. (*Stick a pin in a balloon.*) Have the class predict what the effect might be. After discussing some possible effects, invite a student up to the interactive whiteboard and have the student **drag** the cause through the "Magic Tunnel" so the effect will appear. (*The balloon pops.*) To give the students a visual of cause and effect, direct their attention to the image on the right side of the page.

6. Repeat step 5 with the remaining sentences and images on the page. Discuss the relationship between the causes and effects.

7. Press the arrow to **advance** to the next page. Remind the class that they have been studying the American Indian tribes that lived in the Northwest part of the United States.

Comprehension Activities

Cause and Effect *(cont.)*

Procedure *(cont.)*

8. Read the first cause to the class and have them record it on their activity sheets. Discuss some possible effects that could have taken place because of the cause. In this example,` there could be more than one correct answer as long as the student can justify it.

9. Invite a student up to the interactive whiteboard to **drag** the effect through the "Magic Tunnel" to reveal a possible effect. Have students record these on their activity sheets.

10. Repeat steps 8 and 9 until all of the effects have been revealed.

Possible Lesson Ideas

The following lesson suggestions can accompany this comprehension activity:

- In groups of four, have students create their own totem pole using brown construction paper, empty gallon milk cartons, and a yard stick. Draw symbols on the paper, wrap it around the carton, cut a sliver on the bottom of the milk carton, and slide them through the yard stick.

- Investigate other American Indian tribes that lived in different parts of the United States. Assign groups of students to create *Microsoft PowerPoint*® presentations about the various tribes and share them with the class. Look for similarities and differences among the tribes.

- Create houses of the Northwest using craft sticks or tongue depressors.

Interactive Whiteboard File

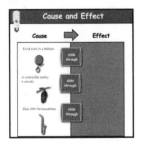 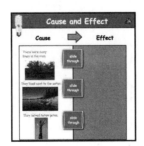

Comprehension Activities

Name: _____

Causes and Effects

Directions: Record the causes and effects on the chart below according to the directions from your teacher.

Cause	Effect

Classify and Categorize

Materials

- Level 3 Interactive Whiteboard File (level3.notebook)
- *So Many Triangles!* activity (p. 85)
- construction paper
- scissors
- glue sticks

Interactive Whiteboard Skills

- Advancing pages
- Dragging objects or text
- Using the eraser
- Using the pen tool

Procedure

1. Launch the Level 3 Notebook file by double-clicking on the icon from the Teacher Resource CD. Press the arrow next to Comprehension activities. Begin this activity by pressing on the Classify and Categorize title from the list.

2. Press the arrow to **advance** to the first activity page on the interactive whiteboard and distribute copies of the *So Many Triangles!* activity sheet (p. 85) to students. Allow students time to cut out the triangles.

3. Tell the class that they are going to try to classify triangles into three categories. Tell them they are going to look at each triangle to see if there are some that have the same characteristics.

4. Have students work with partners to classify the triangles. Try not to give too much help to your students; let them discover classifications on their own. Do not suggest names for the categories at this point. Have students move their triangles on their desks into three separate categories.

5. Invite a pair of students up to the interactive whiteboard to **drag** the triangles on the board into categories according to how they were sorted and to use the **pen tool** to write the category names at the top of the chart. As a class, discuss how the triangles were sorted and have pairs raise their hands if they sorted the same way.

6. **Drag** the triangles out of the chart and use the **eraser** to **erase** the text within the chart. Invite one or two other pairs to repeat steps 5 and 6.

7. Press the arrow to **advance** to the next page. Distribute a sheet of construction paper to each student and have students fold the paper into thirds.

8. Read the categories at the top of the chart and have students label their papers the same way. Then allow students time to look at the angle relationships among the triangles.

Comprehension Activities

Classify and Categorize *(cont.)*

Procedure *(cont.)*

9. Invite a student to the interactive whiteboard to **drag** the acute angles into the correct section. Have students do the same with their triangles and glue them to the construction paper. Repeat this procedure for the remaining two sections.

10. As a class, create class definitions for the three types of triangles and use the **pen tool** to record them in the correct sections on the chart. Have students also record the definitions on the construction paper in the appropriate sections.

Possible Lesson Ideas

The following lesson suggestions can accompany this comprehension activity:

- To review the types of triangles, give each student some uncooked spaghetti. Instruct students to make the three different triangles and glue them to a piece of construction paper.

- Create a triangle book, shaped like a triangle. Have students write about real-life triangles they see or cut out pictures of actual triangles and label them according to the types of angles in the triangles.

- Use what students know about the angles in triangles to investigate the types of angles in other shapes (e.g., *four right angles in a square, six obtuse angles in a regular hexagon*).

Interactive Whiteboard File

So Many Triangles!

Directions: Cut out the triangles below. Sort them according to the directions from your teacher.

Comprehension Activities

Definition: _____

_____
_____
_____
_____

Definition: _____

_____
_____
_____
_____

Definition: _____

_____
_____
_____
_____

Main Idea and Details

Materials

- Level 3 Interactive Whiteboard File (level3.notebook)
- *A Look at the Solar System* activity sheet (p. 88)

Procedure

1. Launch the Level 3 Notebook file by double-clicking on the icon from the Teacher Resource CD. Press the arrow next to Comprehension activities. Begin this activity by pressing on the Main Idea and Details title from the list.

2. Press the arrow to **advance** to the first activity page on the interactive whiteboard and distribute copies of the *A Look at the Solar System* activity sheet (p. 88) to students.

3. Have a student read the title of the passage to the class.

4. Depending on the levels of your students, choose how to best read the text aloud (e.g., echo read, choral read, teacher reads aloud independently, or student volunteers read aloud independently). Read the complete text with students.

5. As a class, decide what is the main idea of the text. Ask a student to **highlight** the sentence that tells the main idea of the passage (*There are many objects that make up our solar system and orbit the sun*). ***Note:*** Press the back arrow to **return** to the first page of text if necessary.

Interactive Whiteboard Skills

- Advancing pages
- Using dual page display
- Using the highlighting tool
- Using the pen tool
- Using the text tool

6. Press the arrow to **advance** to the next page after the text. Use the **pen tool** or the **text tool** to write the main idea at the top of the organizer. Have students record the main idea on their activity sheets, as well.

7. Press the back arrow to **return** to the previous page, or use the **dual page display** to show two pages at once. Read the second paragraph aloud to the class. Discuss the paragraph with the class and see if there are any details that support the main idea. Use the **pen tool** or the **highlighting tool** to underline or **highlight** the supporting details.

8. Press the arrow to **advance** to the next page. Use the **pen tool** or the **text tool** to write a supporting detail at the bottom of the organizer. Have students record the supporting detail on their activity sheets, as well.

Main Idea and Details (cont.)

Procedure (cont.)

9. Repeat steps 6 and 7 to choose two other supporting details from the passage.

10. Have students work with partners to orally summarize the passage using the main ideas and supporting details from their activity sheets.

Possible Lesson Ideas

The following lesson suggestions can accompany this comprehension activity:

*   Present four pictures to students and have them use the pictures to create a story. Have students work with partners to switch stories and identify the main idea and supporting details of the stories.

*   Have students go outside and record what they see in the sky. That same night, have students observe what they see at night. The next day, have students share and chart their observations.

*   Allow students to create Our Solar System books. Have them make tabs on the side of their books to divide their books into sections. As they learn new information, allow them time to record it in their books.

Interactive Whiteboard File

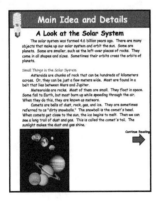 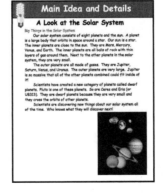 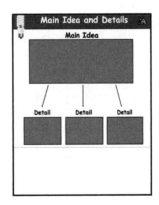

 # A Look at the Solar System

Directions: Add the main idea and supporting details from the passage read aloud in class.

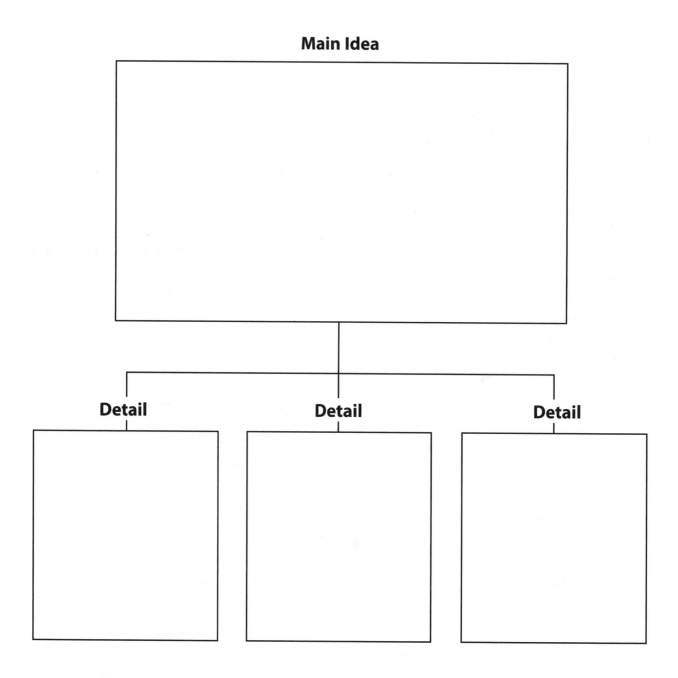

Main Idea

Detail

Detail

Detail

Sequencing

Materials

- Level 3 Interactive Whiteboard File (level3.notebook)
- *Order Matters* activity sheet (p. 91)

Interactive Whiteboard Skills

- Advancing pages
- Dragging objects or text
- Using the highlighting tool
- Using the pen tool
- Using the text tool

Procedure

1. Launch the Level 3 Notebook file by double-clicking on the icon from the Teacher Resource CD. Press the arrow next to Comprehension activities. Begin this activity by pressing on the Sequencing title from the list.

2. Press the arrow to **advance** to the first activity page on the interactive whiteboard and distribute copies of the *Order Matters* activity sheet (p. 91) to students.

3. Ask students to name all of the transition words they know. Use the **pen tool** or the **text tool** to create a list of those words in the box on the interactive whiteboard (possible words include: *to begin, first, second, third, fourth, then, next, and then, after that, finally, lastly, to conclude*).

4. Press the arrow to **advance** to the next page. Read the paragraph aloud to the students. Have them listen for transition words as you read.

5. Invite student volunteers up to the interactive whiteboard to use the **highlighting tool** to highlight the transition words found in the paragraph. If the paragraph uses words that were not included on the original list, press the arrow to **return** to the previous page and add them to the list.

6. Press the arrow to **advance** to the next page. Tell the class that they are going to use this sequence chart to help put the events of the paragraph in the correct order.

7. Invite a student up to the interactive whiteboard and have him or her **drag** the yellow star to the right to reveal an event from the paragraph. Discuss as a class where the event should be placed on the sequencing chart. Remind the students that they may decide to move the event later.

Comprehension Activities

Sequencing *(cont.)*

Procedure *(cont.)*

8. Repeat step 7 until all of the events have been placed on the sequencing chart. If students are struggling, press the arrow to **return** to the previous page and have students read the paragraph again. Once the chart is complete, have students complete their activity sheets.

Possible Lesson Ideas

The following lesson suggestions can accompany this comprehension activity:

- Have students draw images on flash cards of a story they have read. Have students swap cards to see if they can place their partners' cards in the correct sequence.
- Divide the class into groups. After reading a story to the class, place the events of the story on different pieces of paper, one event per sheet. Give one event to each student in the group. Have the group work together to stand in the correct sequence.

Interactive Whiteboard File

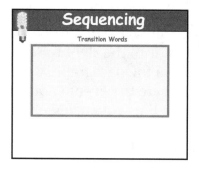
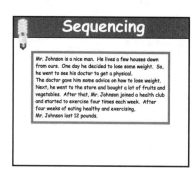
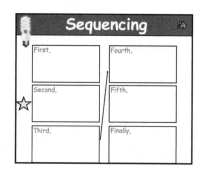

Order Matters

Directions: Place the events in order according to the story read aloud to the class.

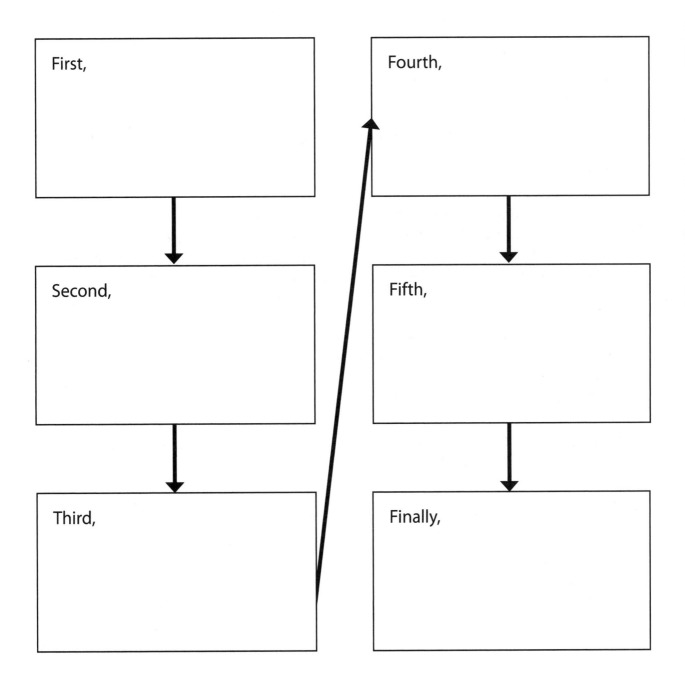

First,

Second,

Third,

Fourth,

Fifth,

Finally,

Comprehension Activities

Summarizing

Materials

- Level 3 Interactive Whiteboard File (level3.notebook)
- *Story Summary* activity sheet (p. 94)
- short, familiar piece of children's literature
- sheet of paper

Interactive Whiteboard Skills

- Advancing pages
- Using the pen tool
- Using the spotlight tool
- Using the text tool

Procedure

1. Launch the Level 3 Notebook file by double-clicking on the icon from the Teacher Resource CD. Press the arrow next to Comprehension activities. Begin this activity by pressing on the Summarizing title from the list.

2. Press the arrow to **advance** to the first activity page on the interactive whiteboard and distribute copies of the *Story Summary* activity sheet (p. 94) to students.

3. Introduce the selected piece of children's literature and then read it aloud to students.

4. Review the different parts of the summary chart with students. Reread the story and have students fill in parts of their activity sheets as they hear them discussed in the story.

5. As a class, discuss each section of the chart. Use the **pen tool** or the **text tool** to record students' ideas. Allow students to edit their charts throughout the class discussion.

6. Review the completed chart using the **spotlight tool** to point out each section of the chart.

7. Have the students use the summary chart to write a one-paragraph summary of the story on their own papers. Invite students to share their completed summaries orally with the class.

Summarizing *(cont.)*

Possible Lesson Ideas

The following lesson suggestions can accompany this comprehension activity:

- After reading a story to the class, have them work in partners as newscasters presenting their summaries to the class as if they are reporters on television.
- Read a chapter book to the class and assign each chapter to a student. The student will draw a picture of the most important event in his or her chapter and write a summary for that chapter. Once everyone is done with his or her summary, create a class book.

Interactive Whiteboard File

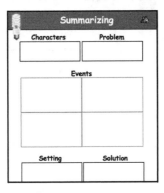

Story Summary

Directions: Complete the chart below to summarize the story that was read aloud to the class.

Characters

Problem

Events

Setting

Solution

Content Links

Materials

- Level 3 Interactive Whiteboard File (level3.notebook)
- *Linking Ideas* activity sheet (p. 97)
- index cards
- marker

Interactive Whiteboard Skills

- Advancing pages
- Dragging objects or text
- Using the pen tool

Procedure

1. Launch the Level 3 Notebook file by double-clicking on the icon from the Teacher Resource CD. Press the arrow next to Review activities. Begin this activity by pressing on the Content Links title from the list.

2. Prior to the activity, write the terms from the first activity page on the index cards, one term per card. There should be one term for each student in the class.

3. Press the arrow to **advance** to the first activity page on the interactive whiteboard and tell the class they are going to do a review activity on the life cycle of a plant. The students should be familiar with these terms before starting this review activity. For struggling students or English language learners, review the terms with drawings or gestures.

4. Distribute one index card to each student.

5. Have each student read his or her term out loud. Discuss the term with the class and review its meaning.

6. Tell students they will circulate around the room with their term looking for another student whose term that has a connection or a link with theirs. Remind the class that there is more than one right answer. Once students choose a person with whom to link, have them discuss how and why their terms are linked together.

7. Have students come up to the interactive whiteboard and **drag** their terms together so they are now "linked" on the board, and use the **pen tool** to write their initials next to their linked terms. After they have "linked" their terms together, have them sit or stand together until the rest of the class has finished linking the terms.

8. Have each pair share out their terms and why they chose to link their terms together. Some students may not find a person with whom to link. Have them stand alone and tell the class why their term could not be linked. As a class, decide how their terms could be linked to make groups of three terms. Mirror those choices on the interactive whiteboard.

Review Activities

Content Links *(cont.)*

Procedure *(cont.)*

9. Once all the groups have had a chance to share, collect the index cards and have students return to their desks. Distribute copies of the *Linking Ideas* activity sheet (p. 97) to students. Have students choose one linked pair from the interactive whiteboard and write the terms in the boxes at the top of the page. Allow them time to write at least four sentences about how those terms are alike and how they are different.

10. To have students play again, **drag** the terms apart on the interactive whiteboard and distribute the index cards again. Tell the class they are going to do the same activity but with a different term. Remind them that they may not link with the same term from the previous round. Repeat steps 6–8 with the class. As a group, discuss why the same terms can be linked in different ways.

Possible Lesson Ideas

The following lesson suggestions can accompany this review activity:

- Soak a seed for each student overnight. The next day, pass out the seeds and have students locate and identify the different parts of the seeds. Have them take off the seed coat, the seed leaf, the embryo, and the hilum, tape these parts into a notebook and label them.

- Have students bring in different plants, fruits, or seeds and investigate their characteristics. Allow them time to compare and contrast the seeds using a Venn diagram. Students can glue the seeds to the diagram.

- Distribute magazines that contain pictures of plants. Have students cut out pictures and glue them onto a piece of construction paper. Then have students investigate the traits that the flowers have in common and the traits that are different.

Interactive Whiteboard File

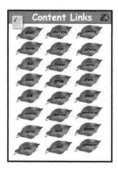

Review Activities

Linking Ideas

Directions: Choose two linked terms from the interactive whiteboard and write them in the boxes below. Write at least four sentences about how the terms are alike and how they are different.

Term:

Term:

_____

_____

_____

_____

_____

_____

_____

_____

_____

Review Activities

Game Board

Materials

- Level 3 Interactive Whiteboard File (level3.notebook)
- *Review Game* activity sheet (p. 100)

Interactive Whiteboard Skills

- Advancing pages
- Dragging objects or text

Procedure

1. Launch the Level 3 Notebook file by double-clicking on the icon from the Teacher Resource CD. Press the arrow next to Review activities. Begin this activity by pressing on the Game Board title from the list.

2. Tell the class that they are going to do an activity to help them review the parts of speech. The students should already have an understanding of the different parts of speech and have had some practice in identifying them and applying them in sentences.

3. Press the arrow to **advance** to the first activity page on the interactive whiteboard and divide the class into five groups. Distribute copies of the *Review Game* activity sheet (p. 100) to each student.

4. Press the spinner in the upper left corner to demonstrate how to make it spin. Spin the spinner and review the part of speech that it lands on. Ask for some examples and use them in a sentence. Do this for all four parts of speech (*adverb, adjective, noun, verb*).

5. Tell students that they will be working together in teams. Their goal is to move their game pieces (space shuttle, jet, motorcycle, helicopter, or car) from the "Start" area to the "Finish" flag. They must also use their charts to record the parts of speech that are landed on throughout the game.

6. To start the game, assign each group a game piece that is on the interactive whiteboard. That game piece will represent their table or group. Select a student from the first group up to the interactive whiteboard.

7. Have the student press the spinner. Once the spinner stops, have the student confer with his or her group to find the first example of the part of speech the spinner landed on. Provide the group with about 20 seconds in which to come to consensus. Then have the student **drag** his or her group's assigned game piece to the first example along the path. For example, if the spinner lands on "Verb," the student will **drag** the game piece to the word *walk*.

Game Board *(cont.)*

Procedure *(cont.)*

8. Have the class decide whether the group moved to the correct space. Then have the class record the chosen word on their activity sheets. In the example above, students would record the word *walk* in the "Verb" column.

9. Select a student from the second group to come up to the interactive whiteboard and press the spinner. Have this group follow the same procedure as the first group to determine where to move its game piece. Continue with the rest of the groups, going in the same order.

10. To win the game, the group must reach the "Finish" flag. If the group spins the spinner and there are no more parts of speech in front of them, they will cross to the "Finish" and win the game. Another way to play is for the groups to go up to the "Finish" and back to the "Start" to win.

Possible Lesson Ideas

The following lesson suggestions can accompany this review activity:

- Distribute blank game boards and have the students create their own games by adding their own examples of the different parts of speech. Have students play each other's games as a center or workstation activity.

- Have students read a short passage of text. Then assign the different parts of speech a color and have students identify the parts of speech used in the passage. For example, have students circle the nouns in blue, underline the verbs in purple, draw a square around the adjectives in red, and draw triangles around the adverbs in yellow.

Interactive Whiteboard File

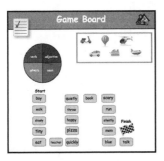

Review Activities

Review Game

Directions: Once a team lands on a word, record it in the correct category in the chart below.

Noun	Verb	Adjective	Adverb

Review Activities

Guess It!

Materials

- Level 3 Interactive Whiteboard File (level3.notebook)
- *Guess It!* activity sheet (p. 103)
- ballpoint pens or markers

Interactive Whiteboard Skills

- Advancing pages
- Dragging objects or text
- Using the screen shade

Procedure

1. Launch the Level 3 Notebook file by double-clicking on the icon from the Teacher Resource CD. Press the arrow next to Review activities. Begin this activity by pressing on the Guess It! title from the list.

2. Tell the class that they are going to do an activity to help them review the locations of cities and states. Students should already have an understanding of the states and major cities within the United States.

3. Press the arrow to **advance** to the first activity page on the interactive whiteboard and distribute copies of the *Guess It!* activity sheet (p. 103) to students. Also distribute a ballpoint pen or marker to each student.

4. Slide the **screen shade** down until it reveals the first clue to the class (*I am a state*). Read the clue aloud and tell students that this is their first clue to help them guess the name of a state. Have students guess which state it might be and then write that down on their activity sheets next to number "1."

5. Once all the students have written down a guess, select some of the students to share out their guesses to the class. (Students use pens so that they cannot erase and change their guesses.) Now slide the **screen shade** down until the second clue is revealed to the class (*My last letter is an "a"*).

6. Select a student to read the first two clues to the class. Instruct students to record another guess, this time next to number "2." If a student does not want to change his or her guess, have the student write the same state on the paper next to number "2." Once all the students have taken another guess, select some of the students to share out their guesses. Ask the students why they decided to change their guess.

7. Repeat step 6 until all of the clues are revealed.

8. **Drag** the **screen shade** all the way to the bottom of the page to reveal the picture of the state (*Indiana*).

Guess It! *(cont.)*

Procedure *(cont.)*

9. Press the arrow to **advance** to the next page. Repeat the review game using steps 4–9.

Possible Lesson Ideas

The following lesson suggestions can accompany this review activity:

- Have students select their own city or state and have them find seven facts about it. Students are going to create their own *Guess It!* using those seven facts. Remind students to place their clues in order from very broad to very specific.
- Have students create a state or city report. It can be a written report or a multi-media report utilizing photos, videos, music, and other types of digital media.

Interactive Whiteboard File

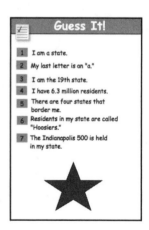

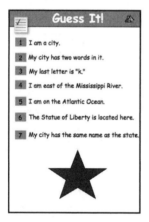

Review Activities

Guess It!

Directions: Read the clues displayed on the board. Record your guesses below.

1. _____

2. _____

3. _____

4. _____

5. _____

6. _____

7. _____

Which state am I? _____

1. _____

2. _____

3. _____

4. _____

5. _____

6. _____

7. _____

Which state am I? _____

Review Activities

Question It!

Materials

- Level 3 Interactive Whiteboard File (level3.notebook)
- *Question It! Recording Sheet* (p. 106)

Interactive Whiteboard Skills

- Advancing pages
- Dragging objects or text

Procedure

1. Launch the Level 3 Notebook file by double-clicking on the icon from the Teacher Resource CD. Press the arrow next to Review activities. Begin this activity by pressing on the Question It! title from the list.

2. Tell the class that they are going to do an activity to help them review math skills they have been studying. The students should already have an understanding of single-digit multiplication, perimeter, and expressions using word problems.

3. Press the arrow to **advance** to the first activity page on the interactive whiteboard and distribute copies of the *Question It! Recording Sheet* (p. 106) to students.

4. Invite a student up to the interactive whiteboard to select a category and a value. Tell the students that the easier questions have lower values, and the higher valued questions are the more difficult questions.

5. Have the student select a question by pushing on the number (e.g., *200*). The question will appear. Although only one student can select a question, instruct every student to copy and solve the question at the bottom of his or her activity sheet. Then have each student write the letter of the correct answer in the corresponding cell of the question grid.

6. Allow students time to answer the question. Then reveal the answer by **dragging** the yellow box located in the bottom right hand corner to the red X located in the bottom left hand corner. The correct answer will be circled so all students can check their work. Discuss the answer as a class.

7. If the student has the correct answer, have him or her circle the value of the question on his or her recording sheet. For example, students with the correct answer would circle the 200 on the answer sheet in the "Number Sense" column. If the student has the incorrect answer, have the student place a line through the value of the question.

Review Activities

Question It! *(cont.)*

Procedure *(cont.)*

8. Press the Question It! house icon located in the upper right hand corner of the page to return to the Question It! home page. Before selecting another student to the interactive whiteboard, **drag** the red X, which is infinitely cloned, over the question that was just selected so no other student selects that question again.

9. Once all the questions have been answered and reviewed, have students total their points by adding up all of the numbers they have circled on their answer sheets. *Note:* There are two "Daily Double" questions in this game. If a student selects a question and the "Daily Double" page appears, it will double the value of the question. For example, if a student selects a question worth 400, it will be doubled to 800.

Possible Lesson Ideas

The following lesson suggestions can accompany this review activity:

- Have students create their own review questions on 3" × 5" cards. Partner students up or place them in small groups. Have students mix up the cards and turn them over. One student turns a card over and the first student who says the correct answer gets to keep the card. Students try to collect the most cards.

- Place students into small groups and number each student in the group. Place a question on the interactive whiteboard and have each group work together to solve the problem. Have groups record their answers on small dry-erase boards. After the groups have finished, select a number and have students who are assigned that number hold up their boards to reveal their answers. Each group with the correct answer gets a point.

Interactive Whiteboard File

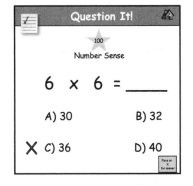

Review Activities

Question It! Recording Sheet

Directions: Use the space below to copy and solve the questions that appear on the board. Write the letter of your answer on the line in the corresponding box below. If your answer is correct, circle the number value in the box. If your answer is incorrect, draw a line through the number value in the box.

Number Sense	Algebra and Function	Measurement and Geometry
_____ 100	_____ 100	_____ 100
_____ 200	_____ 200	_____ 200
_____ 300	_____ 300	_____ 300
_____ 400	_____ 400	_____ 400
_____ 500	_____ 500	_____ 500

Review Activities

Draw and Guess

Materials

- Level 3 Interactive Whiteboard File (level3.notebook)
- *Draw and Guess Recording Sheet* (p. 109)
- timer

Interactive Whiteboard Skills

- Advancing pages
- Dragging objects or text
- Using the eraser tool
- Using the pen tool

Procedure

1. Launch the Level 3 Notebook file by double-clicking on the icon from the Teacher Resource CD. Press the arrow next to Review activities. Begin this activity by pressing on the Draw and Guess title from the list.

2. Tell the class that they are going to do an activity to help them review some basic parts of speech. They will review nouns, verbs, adjectives, and adverbs.

3. Place students into five groups. Press the arrow to **advance** to the first activity page on the interactive whiteboard and distribute copies of the *Draw and Guess Recording Sheet* (p. 109) to students.

4. Invite one student up to the interactive whiteboard from each group. Have each student press the die. The order of play is determined by who rolls the highest number. Instruct the remaining students to return to their groups' areas.

5. Assign a game piece to each group. Have the student press the die and move the game piece marked "1" to the appropriate location on the board.

6. Have the student read which part of speech his or her game piece is on and then press the arrow to **advance** to the next page.

7. **Drag** the pull tab at the top of the page up to remind the students the definition of the corresponding part of speech. Have the student whisper something that is in the category that he or she would like to draw. For example, if the group landed on "Noun," the student may choose to draw a dog.

8. Tell the student that he or she has one minute to use the **pen tool** to try to draw the thing he or she chose from the category. Remind the student that he or she may not use any letters, numbers, or symbols on the interactive whiteboard—only images—and that he or she may use the colored pens if desired.

9. Set a timer for one minute. Instruct the student to begin as soon as you start the timer. As the student is drawing the image, allow the other students in the group to call out guesses.

Review Activities

Draw and Guess (cont.)

Procedure (cont.)

10. If no one in the group guesses the image within one minute, then the group will keep its game piece where it is. Have the student share what he or she was drawing. Instruct everyone in the class to write a sentence using the word the student was trying to draw. Use the **eraser tool** to delete the drawing before calling up a student from the next group to take a turn.

11. If someone in the group guesses correctly, allow the group to take another turn. The class must still write a sentence using the word before the group can roll the die again.

12. Press the back arrow to return to the game board to roll the die for the next turn. The first group to get its game piece to the "Finish" wins the game.

Possible Lesson Ideas

The following lesson suggestions can accompany this review activity:

- Have students create their own games. Delete all the parts of speech terms on page one and then print it out for each student. Have students place their own terms on the game board and come up with their own rules. Have students work on writing up the rules and procedures for their game.

Interactive Whiteboard File

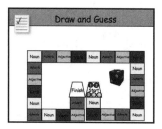

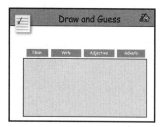

Draw and Guess Recording Sheet

Directions: Write a sentence for each word that was drawn.

1. _____

2. _____

3. _____

4. _____

5. _____

6. _____

7. _____

8. _____

9. _____

10. _____

11. _____

12. _____

13. _____

14. _____

15. _____

Review Activities

Appendices

References Cited

Becker, C. and M. Lee. 2009. *The interactive whiteboard revolution: Teaching with IWBs.* Victoria, Australia: ACER Press.

Beeland Jr., D. 2002. *Student engagement, visual learning and technology: Can interactive whiteboards help?* Available: http://teach.valdosta.edu/are/Artmanscrpt/vol1no1/beeland_am.pdf

Magaña, S. and P. Frenkel. 2009. *Transforming teaching and learning for the 21st century.* Available: http://www.prometheanworld.com/upload/pdf/transforming_Teaching_and_Learnng_for_the_21st_Century_V6_pdf.

Marzano, R. J. 2009. The art and science of teaching: Teaching with interactive whiteboards. *Educational Leadership* 67 (November): 80–82.

Marzano, R. J., and M. Haystead. 2009. *Final report on the evaluation of the Promethean technology.* Englewood, CO: Marzano Research Laboratory.

Torff, B. and R. Tirotta, 2010. Interactive whiteboards produce small gains in elementary students' self-reported motivation in mathematics. *Computers & Education* 54, 370–383.

Literature Cited

White, E. B. *Charlotte's Web.* New York: HarperCollins, 1980.

Answer Key

Scrambled Up (p. 22)

  1. pickle, mustard, ketchup, Condiments Used on a Hamburger

  2. vanilla, chocolate, strawberry, Flavors of Ice Cream

Understanding Analogies (p. 25)

  1. Gas is to car as soil is to flower

  2. Kittens are to cats as seeds are to plants

  3. Arm is to body as leaf is to stem

  4. Mail is to mailman as pollen is to bee

My Day (p. 28)

Responses will vary.

Daily Geography (p. 31)

  1. ←; west

  2. →; east

  3. ↑; north

  4. ↓; south

  1. B

  2. A

  3. B

  4. C

Math Practice (p. 34)

  1. 972

  2. $\frac{3}{4}$

  3. 28

  4. 5,477

  5. 45

  6. 15 in.

  7. 3,410

  8. pentagon

  9. 3,800

Alike and Different (p. 37)

  1. Responses will vary.

  2. Responses will vary.

Answer Key *(cont.)*

Concept of Definition Map (p. 40)
Responses depend on class discussion.

Example/Nonexample (p. 43)
Solid:
Examples: apple, desk, hat, ice cube
Nonexamples: milk, water, soda, oxygen
Liquid:
Examples: coffee, milk, water
Nonexample: calculator, pencil, truck

Shape Actions (p. 46)

Shape	Number of Sides	Number of Vertices	Example	Action
triangle	3	3	Responses will depend on class discussion.	Action will depend on class discussion.
quadrilateral	4	4	Responses will depend on class discussion.	Action will depend on class discussion.
pentagon	5	5	Responses will depend on class discussion.	Action will depend on class discussion.
hexagon	6	6	Responses will depend on class discussion.	Action will depend on class discussion.
octagon	8	8	Responses will depend on class discussion.	Action will depend on class discussion.

Understanding Prefixes (p. 49)
re- "again"; Possible words: redo, reappear, replay, rewrite
un- "not"; Possible words: unclog, unable, unlucky, undo
dis- "not or opposite"; Possible words: dishonest, disapprove, disappear, disable
mis- "wrong"; Possible words: misjudge, misspell, mismatch
  1. remove
  2. misplaced
  3. untie
  4. dislike

Analyze This! (p. 52)
Responses will vary.

Answer Key *(cont.)*

Anticipation Guide (p. 55)
Responses will vary.

Stay In School (p. 58)
1. $17.25 more per week
2. The trained and educated worker earns more money.
3. Responses will vary.
4. Responses will vary.

Water, Anyone? (p. 61)
Groupings will vary.

Adjective Predictions (p. 64)
Responses will vary.

Comparing Sports (p. 67)
Responses will vary.

How to Make... (p. 70)
1. Find the bread, peanut butter, and jelly .
2. Spread peanut butter on one slice of bread.
3. Spread jelly on the other slice.
4. Press the slices of bread together.
5. Cut sandwich
6. Enjoy with milk!

My KWL (p. 73)
Responses will vary.

Answer Key *(cont.)*

Representing Numbers (p. 76)

Numeral	Base-Ten Blocks	Expanded Form
452		400 + 50 + 2
625		600 + 20 + 5
1,237		1,000 + 200 + 30 + 7
2,680		2,000 + 600 + 80
4,006		4,000 + 6

Answer Key *(cont.)*

Landform Web (p. 79)

Responses will include ocean, lake, mountain, river, and valley.

Causes and Effects (p. 82)

Cause: There were many trees in the area; Possible Effect: They made their homes out of logs.

Cause: They lived next to the water; Possible Effect: They ate many types of seafood.

Cause: They carved totem poles; Possible Effect: Told a story about the family.

So Many Triangles! (p. 85)

Acute	Obtuse	Right

A Look at the Solar System (p. 88)

Main Idea: There are many things that make up our Solar System and that orbit the Sun.

Details: Responses will vary.

Order Matters (p. 91)

First, Mr. Johnson decided to lose weight.

Second, he went to see his doctor to get a physical.

Third, the doctor gave him some advice on how to lose weight.

Fourth, he went to the store and bought fruits and vegetables.

Fifth, Mr. Johnson joined a health club and started to exercise.

Last, Mr. Johnson lost 12 pounds in four weeks.

Story Summary (p. 94)

Responses will vary.

Linking Ideas (p. 97)

Links will vary.

Review Game (p. 100)

Answers will vary.

Guess It! (p. 103)

1. Indiana
2. New York

Answer Key *(cont.)*

Question It! Recording Sheet (p. 106)

Question It! Answers			
	Number Sense	**Algebra and Function**	**Measurement and Geometry**
100	B	B	A
200	C	A	D
300	A	C	D
400	D	B	C
500	B	C	D

Draw and Guess Recording Sheet (p. 109)

Sentences will vary.

Content-Area Matrix

Content Area	Activity Title
Mathematics	• Daily Mathematics • Total Physical Response • Historical Document • T-Chart • Classify and Categorize • Question It!
Science	• Analogies • Example/Nonexample • List, Group, Label • KWL Chart • Main Idea and Details • Content Links
Social Studies	• Daily Geography • Concept of Definition Map • Analyze the Picture • Web Map • Cause and Effect • Guess It!
Reading	• Anagram Words • Alike and Different • Anticipation Guide • Flow Chart • Sequencing • Draw and Guess
Writing	• Calendar • Word Tiles • Picture Predictions • Venn Diagram • Summarizing • Game Board

How-to Guide

Advancing pages

1. When in slideshow view on the interactive whiteboard, press the forward arrow from the toolbar.

2. In full screen view, press the forward arrow on the floating toolbar.

3. If you want to move to the previous page, press the backward arrow.

4. To return to the home menu page, press the house icon on the top of the page.

1.    2.    4.

Saving a file

1. When viewing a file on a computer, select **File** from the menu across the top of the page.

2. Then select *Save*.

3. When viewing the file on an interactive whiteboard, select the cursor tool from the toolbar.

4. Then press the *Save* icon on the toolbar.

2. 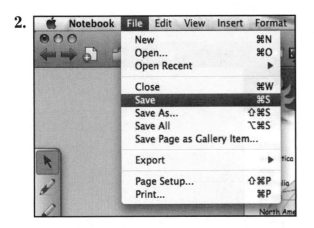   3.    4.

How-to Guide *(cont.)*

Dragging objects or text

1. Select the cursor tool from the toolbar.

2. Press on the desired object or piece of text.

3. Without lifting your finger, drag the object or text to the desired location.

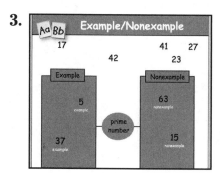

Using the eraser

1. Select the eraser tool from the toolbar.

2. Choose the width of the eraser by pressing the desired box with your finger.

3. Pick up the eraser tool from the shelf on the interactive whiteboard. Use it like a regular eraser to delete the desired text or drawings. *Note:* The eraser will only remove information recorded with the pen tool.

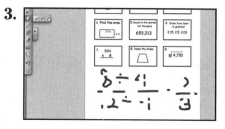

Using the highlighting tool

1. Select the pen tool from the toolbar.

2. Select either the yellow highlighter or the green highlighter from the menu by pressing the desired box with your finger.

3. Highlight desired text by dragging the pen over the text.

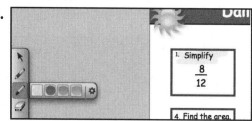

How-to Guide *(cont.)*

Using the pen tool

1. Select the pen tool from the toolbar.

2. Select a color or style from the menu by pressing the desired box with your finger.

3. Write or draw using the pen.

3.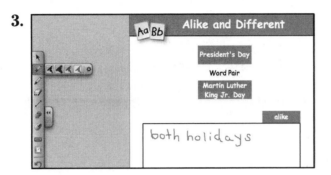

Using the text tool

1. Select the text tool from the toolbar.

2. Select the desired text size.

3. Press anywhere on the screen that you would like text to appear.

4. Type the desired text.

5. Select the cursor tool and grab the text to move it around the page, if desired.

2.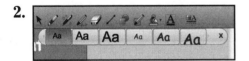

4.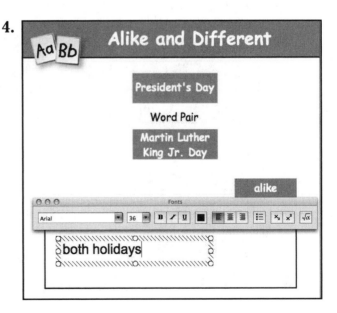

How-to Guide *(cont.)*

Using dual page display

1. Select the dual page display icon from the toolbar. The screen will divide in half and the current page will be displayed on the right.

2. Press the arrow to advance the current page to the left. The next page will appear on the right. The two pages can now be viewed and manipulated side-by-side.

1.

Dual Page Display

Pinning pages

1. Select the dual page display icon from the toolbar. The screen will divide in half and the current page will be displayed on the right.

2. Press the arrow to advance the page you want to be pinned until it appears on the right side of the display.

3. Select the pin page tool from the toolbar. This will pin the current page displayed on the left.

4. If you do not have the pin page tool on your toolbar, use the computer to select **View** from the main toolbar menu, then select **Zoom** from the drop-down menu.

5. Then select *pin page* from the second drop-down menu. This will pin the current page displayed on the left.

1.

Dual Page Display

3.

5.

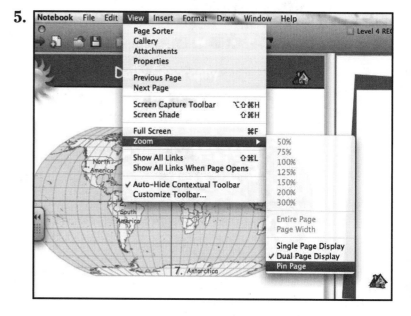

How-to Guide *(cont.)*

Using the cell shade

Note: The cell shade only works when using a table.

1. When viewing a table file on a computer, right click in the cell into which you want to insert the cell shade.

2. Select **Add Cell Shade** from the drop-down menu. The cell shade appears.

3. To remove the cell shade, select the cursor tool from the toolbar then press the cell shade with your finger.

4. When viewing a file on the interactive whiteboard, use the mouse buttons on the front of the interactive whiteboard to right click in the cell into which you want to insert the cell shade. Then repeat steps 2 and 3 above.

2. 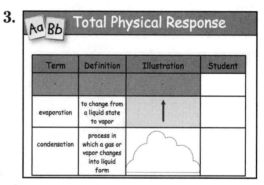 **3.**

Using the screen shade

1. Select the show/hide screen shade tool from the toolbar. A screen shade will appear on the entire screen.

2. Adjust the size of the screen shade by dragging the top or sides of the shade.

3. To reveal the hidden information, drag the desired portion of the screen shade slowly.

4. To remove the shade completely, press the red circle in the top right corner of the shade.

1. 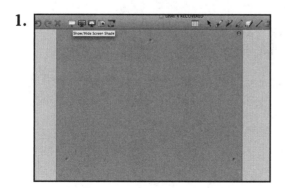 **2.**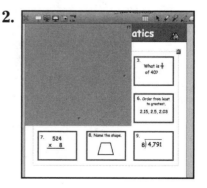

How-to Guide *(cont.)*

Using the spotlight tool

1. Select the spotlight tool from the toolbar. To turn on the **spotlight tool**, select the customize floating tools icon located at the bottom of the vertical tool bar. Then select **Other Interactive Whiteboard Tools** and then ***Spotlight.*** The screen will go dark except for a single circle.

2. To change the size or location of the circle, grab and drag the spotlight using any black portion of the screen.

3. To change the shape of the spotlight, select ***Shape*** from the drop-down menu on the spotlight shown on the screen. Choose the desired shape from the second drop-down menu that appears.

4. To change the transparency of the background, select ***Transparency*** from the drop-down menu on the spotlight shown on the screen. Choose the desired transparency from the second drop-down menu that appears.

4.
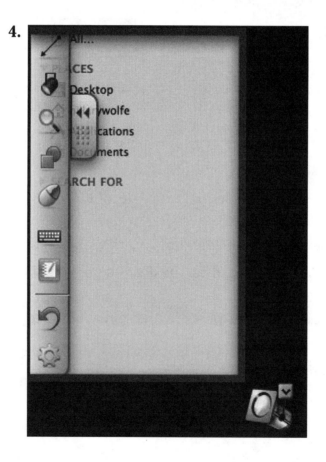

Interactive Whiteboard Skills Matrix

Activity Title	Interactive Whiteboard Skills Used
Anagram Words	• Advancing pages • Dragging objects or text • Using the screen shade
Analogies	• Advancing pages • Dragging objects or text
Calendar	• Advancing pages • Dragging objects or text • Using the pen tool
Daily Geography	• Advancing pages • Dragging objects or text
Daily Mathematics	• Advancing pages • Dragging objects or text • Using the spotlight tool
Alike and Different	• Advancing pages • Using dual page display • Using the pen tool • Using the text tool
Concept of Definition Map	• Advancing pages • Using the pen tool • Using the text tool
Example/Nonexample	• Advancing pages • Dragging objects or text • Using the pen tool • Using the text tool
Total Physical Response	• Advancing pages • Using the cell shade • Using the pen tool • Using the text tool
Word Tiles	• Advancing pages • Dragging objects or text
Analyze the Picture	• Advancing pages • Dragging objects or text

Interactive Whiteboard Skills Matrix *(cont.)*

Activity Title	Interactive Whiteboard Skills Used
Anticipation Guide	• Advancing pages • Dragging objects or text • Using the pen tool
Historical Document	• Advancing pages • Dragging objects or text • Using the spotlight tool
List, Group, Label	• Advancing pages • Dragging objects or text • Using the text tool
Picture Predictions	• Advancing pages • Dragging objects or text • Using the pen tool • Using the text tool
Venn Diagram	• Advancing pages • Dragging objects or text • Using the pen tool • Using the text tool
Flow Chart	• Advancing pages • Dragging objects or text
KWL Chart	• Advancing pages • Using the pen tool • Using the screen shade • Using the text tool
T-Chart	• Advancing pages • Dragging objects or text • Using the pen tool
Web Map	• Advancing pages • Dragging objects or text • Using dual page display *(optional)* • Using the pen tool • Using the text tool
Cause and Effect	• Advancing pages • Dragging objects or text

Interactive Whiteboard Skills Matrix *(cont.)*

Activity Title	Interactive Whiteboard Skills Used
Classify and Categorize	• Advancing pages • Dragging objects or text • Using the eraser • Using the pen tool
Main Idea and Details	• Advancing pages • Using dual page display • Using the highlighting tool • Using the pen tool • Using the text tool
Sequencing	• Advancing pages • Dragging objects or text • Using the highlighting tool • Using the pen tool • Using the text tool
Summarizing	• Advancing pages • Using the pen tool • Using the spotlight tool • Using the text tool
Content Links	• Advancing pages • Dragging objects or text • Using the pen tool
Game Board	• Advancing pages • Dragging objects or text
Guess It!	• Advancing pages • Dragging objects or text • Using the screen shade
Question It!	• Advancing pages • Dragging objects or text
Draw and Guess	• Advancing pages • Dragging objects or text • Using the eraser tool • Using the pen tool

Contents of the Teacher Resource CD

Teacher Resources

Activity	File Name
Level 3 Interactive Whiteboard Files	level3.notebook
Instructional Time Line	timeline.pdf
How-to Guide	how-to.pdf

Student Reproducibles

Activity	File Name
Scrambled Up	page22.pdf
Understanding Analogies	page25.pdf
My Day	page28.pdf
Daily Geography	page31.pdf
Math Practice	page34.pdf
Vocabulary Development Activities	
Alike and Different	page37.pdf
Concept of Definition Map	page40.pdf
Example/Nonexample	page43.pdf
Shape Actions	page46.pdf
Understanding Prefixes	page49.pdf
Activating Prior Knowledge Activities	
Analyze This!	page52.pdf
Anticipation Guide	page55.pdf
Stay in School	page58.pdf
Water, Anyone?	page61.pdf
Adjective Predictions	page64.pdf
Graphic Organizer Activities	
Comparing Sports	page67.pdf
How to Make…	page70.pdf
My KWL	page73.pdf
Representing Numbers	page76.pdf
Landform Web	page79.pdf
Comprehension Activities	
Causes and Effects	page82.pdf
So Many Triangles!	page85.pdf
A Look at the Solar System	page88.pdf
Order Matters	page91.pdf
Story Summary	page94.pdf
Review Activities	
Linking Ideas	page97.pdf
Review Game	page100.pdf
Guess It!	page103.pdf
Question It! Recording Sheet	page106.pdf
Draw and Guess Recording Sheet	page109.pdf